Nick Smethurst is a proud dad of two boys

Raised in Manchester, he is a proud Northern... ...lieve he has a good sense of humour, his friends would disagree!

Nick never intended on writing a book but the Covid lockdowns in the UK allowed him to start posting on social media about one of his passions, Idioms/sayings/phrases and their origins.

Nick quickly realised he wasn't on his own with his fascination and after posting well over 300 of these 'origin' stories he gained a large following of people who would get involved by posing new ones to Nick.

After several calls for him to collect all the stories into one document Nick decided to see if any publishers would be interested in working with him to create the book you have in your hands now.

Nick's idiom journey still continues on social media and he has hopes to bring you the second instalment…watch this space.

I would like to dedicate this book to my children – Jake Smethurst & Isaac Smethurst, who along with me are pictured in the illustrations.

Nick Smethurst

AN IDIOT'S LOVE
OF IDIOMS

AUSTIN MACAULEY PUBLISHERS™

LONDON · CAMBRIDGE · NEW YORK · SHARJAH

A CIP catalogue record for this title is available from the British Library.

ISBN 9781398470859(Paperback)
ISBN 9781398470866 (ePub e-book)

www.austinmacauley.com

First Published 2022
Austin Macauley Publishers Ltd®
1 Canada Square
Canary Wharf
London
E14 5AA

Special thanks to Timothy M Jones who gave me the confidence to collect the idioms and even wrote to publishers for me.
I probably wouldn't have wrote this book without him telling me it was worth it.

I would also like to credit the illustrator – Peter Van Der Merwe.

Special thanks also go to all the people who follow me on LinkedIn for reading the idioms weekly.

Table of Contents

"Cat Got Your Tongue"

Meaning: Said to someone who remains silent when they are expected to speak.
Origin: There are two stories on how this saying came into being. The first one says that it could have come from a whip called 'Cat-o'-nine-tails' that was used by the English Navy for flogging and often left the victims speechless.
The second one may be from ancient Egypt, where liars' tongues were cut out as punishment and fed to the cats.
There is no definitive evidence that these are where the saying comes from however, and there are no printed examples pre-mid-nineteenth century. So the saying may not be as old as one might think, as in this example from the Wisconsin newspaper 'The Racine Democrat', December 1859:

"How I love a rainy day!" he said. To this, I made no answer. I loved a rainy day too, but I was not disposed to say so just then. "Oh ho! The cat got your tongue, has it?" was his next remark.

"The Walls Have Ears"

Meaning: Be careful what you say as people may be eavesdropping.
Origin: Experts believe this saying may come from a story about Dionysius of Syracuse (430–367 BC), who had an ear-shaped cave cut and connected between the rooms of his palace so that he could hear what was being said from another room.
Another story, however, was about the Louvre Palace in France, which was believed to have a network of listening tubes so that it would be possible to hear everything that was said in different rooms. People say that this is how the Queen Catherine de'Medici discovered political secrets and plots around 1620.
In English, the phrase 'the walls have ears' was first recorded in its present form in 1633 in James Shirley's play 'The Bird in a Cage': "Take heed to what I say, the walls have ears."

"My Ears Are Burning"

Meaning: One is subconsciously aware of being talked about or criticised.

Origin: The idiom is ancient and the origin of this belief goes back to Roman times when Augurs (Ancient Roman priest) paid particular attention to such signs. Pliny wrote in 'Naturalis Historia' (AD 77):

"It is acknowledged that the absent feel a presentiment of remarks about themselves by the ringing of their ears."

The ancient belief that the left signifies evil and the right good applies here also. Both Plautus and Pliny held that if a person's right ear burns then he is being praised, but a burning left ear indicates that he is the subject of evil intent. English literature, from Chaucer to Dickens, abounds with references to burning ears.

"Bury the Hatchet"

Meaning: End a quarrel or conflict and become friendly.

Origin: The phrase, bury the hatchet, comes from a ceremony performed by Native Americans when previously warring tribes declared peace. When two tribes decided to settle their differences and live in harmony, the chief of each tribe buried a war hatchet in the ground to signify their agreement.

Europeans became aware of this ceremony as early as 1644. It is certain that the ceremony of burying the hatchet, however, had been practiced for many years before the arrival of the Europeans. So, although the saying is mid -seventeenth century, the act in itself is probably much older.

"Cold Feet"

Meaning: Loss of nerve or confidence.

Origin: It is believed this idiom originates from an ancient military term, warriors who had frozen feet were not able to rush into battle.

The Oxford English Dictionary attributes the earliest printed usage of 'cold feet' in this sense to the writer and poet Stephen Crane. In the second edition of 'Maggie: A Girl of the Streets', published in 1896:

"I knew this was the way it would be. They got cold feet." That is, they lost courage or enthusiasm.

By the early 1900s, the phrase was being used wide spread. A few years later, the term 'cold-footer' was applied to those who were afraid to fight in the First World War.

"Big Wig"

Meaning: An important person, especially in a particular sphere.

Origin: The fashion for wigs began with the Kings of France. Louis XIII (1601–1643) went prematurely bald and took to wearing a wig. By the middle of the century, and especially during the reign of Louis XIV, known as the Sun King, wigs were virtually obligatory for all European nobility and 'persons of quality'. At that time, they were known in England as periwigs, which was shortened to wig by 1675.

The earliest discovered record of this in print is G. Selwyn's 1781 Letters:

"A new point of discussion for the lawyers, for our big wigs, for their Lordships."

"Don't Look a Gift Horse in the Mouth"

Meaning: Find fault with something that has been received as a gift or favour.

Origin: Many years ago people would determine a horse's age and condition based on its teeth, and then decide whether they would want to buy it or not. This is the reason why people use this idiom, to say it is rude to look for flaws in a thing that was given to you as a gift.

This is also where 'Long in the tooth' comes from as the longer the tooth because of receding gums would show the age and quality of a horse.

The phrase first appears in print in English in John Heywood's 'A Dialogue Conteinyng the Nomber in Effect of all the Prouerbes in the Englishe Tongue' (1546) as:

"Don't look a given horse in the mouth."

"Caught Red-Handed"

Meaning: Used to indicate that a person has been discovered in or just after the act of doing something wrong or illegal.

The expression 'caught red handed' has its origins in Scotland around the fifteenth century. Given how it was used in the earliest references, the phrase 'red hand' is thought to refer to people caught with blood on their hands from murder or poaching. Many believe there was a law stating that providing there was no blood on the hands of the offender then they could not be brought to justice, this is believed to come from the poaching of livestock, however, there is no printed evidence of this.

The first documented mention of 'red hand' is in the Scottish Acts of Parliament of James I, written in 1432:

"That the offender be taken red hand."

The first documented instance of the expression morphing from 'red hand' to 'red handed' was in the early nineteenth-century work Ivanhoe, written by Sir Walter Scott:

"I did but tie one fellow, who was taken red-handed."

"Blood Is Thicker Than Water"

Meaning: Family relationships and loyalties are the strongest and most important ones.

Origin: Even though many might think this saying means that we should put family ahead of friends, it is believed to originally have actually meant the complete opposite.

The full phrase was actually "The blood of the covenant is thicker than the water of the womb", and it referred to warriors who shared the blood they shed in battles together. These 'blood brothers' were said to have stronger bonds than biological brothers.

The first printed version of this saying is in a German equivalent proverb '*Blut ist dicker als Wasser*' which first appeared in this form in the medieval German epic Reinhart Fuchs in 1180.

By 1670, the modern version was included in John Ray's collected Proverbs, and later appeared in Scottish author John Moore's 'Zeluco' (1789).

"So you see there is little danger of my forgetting them, and far less blood relations; for surely blood is thicker than water."

"Riding Shotgun"

Meaning: Used to claim the right to sit in the front passenger seat of a vehicle on a particular journey.

Origin: This expression refers to the passenger of an old-fashioned stagecoach in the 'cowboy' era, there would be a passenger accompanying the driver with a shotgun to protect from thieves or attackers along the way.

There is nothing in print from this time to suggest the expression was actually used in the 'Wild West', the expression came much later on, when media and films began to romanticise the period. The first known use of the phrase 'riding shotgun' was in the 1905 novel 'The Sunset Trail' by Alfred Henry Lewis.

"Turn a Blind Eye"

Meaning: Pretend not to notice.

Origin: This expression is believed to have been popularised during the siege of Copenhagen (1801), in which Lord Horatio Nelson, Second in Command of the English Fleet, was ordered to withdraw but pretended not to see the flagship's signals. He did this by putting his telescope to the eye that had been blinded in an earlier battle. He attacked, nevertheless, and was victorious.

Although Nelson may well have brought this saying to the fore, we can see a similar example put into print first by the British novelist Francis Lathom in 'Men and Manners' (1800):

"It is lucky for the poor man he has a blind eye to turn to her," cried Lady Varny.

What we can definitively say is the phrase has been used well over 200 years.

"Bite the Bullet"

Meaning: Decide to do something difficult or unpleasant that one has been putting off or hesitating over.

Origin: This phrase was first recorded by Rudyard Kipling in his 1891 novel 'The Light that Failed'. The thought is that it is derived historically from the practice of having a patient clench a bullet in their teeth as a way to cope with the pain of a surgical procedure without anaesthetic.

It is not certain, but is thought to have evolved from the British expression 'to bite the cartridge', which dates back to the Indian Rebellion of 1857, but the phrase 'chew a bullet', with a similar meaning, dates to at least 1796.

"One for the Road"

Meaning: A final drink before leaving a place.

Origin: The theory is that during the middle ages, those condemned to death by execution were taken through what today is known as Oxford Street at the Tyburn tree. During this final trip, the cart would stop and they would be allowed to have one final drink before their death. This may be the case but there is no written evidence.

The phrase itself is of the twentieth century and came into being around the time of the outbreak of the Second World War. However, the 'for the road' element does have its origin in earlier times.

In eighteenth-century England, food outlets would have been few and far in between. If travellers wanted to eat on their journey, they had to take their food with them. Whatever one needed for one's journey was said to be 'for the road'. An early example of that in print can be seen in a journal called 'The Beauties of all the Magazines' (1763):

"The chief shepherd gives them three shillings in April, and three shillings in October, by way of regale for the road."

"Honeymoon"

Meaning: A holiday spent together by a newly married couple.

Origin: The word 'honeymoon' itself is derived from the Scandinavian practice of drinking mead, or fermented honey, during the first month of the marriage, measured by one moon cycle, in order to improve the likelihood of conception. The word also showed up in the 1500s as a term to warn newlyweds about waning love. The message was clear: "As the moon wanes, so shall your love."

"White Elephant"

Meaning: A possession that is useless or troublesome, especially one that is expensive to maintain or difficult to dispose of.

Origin: The term derives from the sacred white elephants kept by Southeast Asian monarchs in Burma, Thailand, Laos and Cambodia. To possess a white elephant was regarded as a sign that the monarch reigned with justice and power. Because the animals were considered sacred and local laws protected them from labour, receiving a gift of a white elephant from a monarch was simultaneously a blessing and a curse. It was a blessing because the animal was sacred and a sign of the monarch's favour, and a curse because the recipient now had an expensive animal he could not give away.

In the West, the term 'white elephant' meaning an expensive burden that fails to meet expectations, was first used in the 1600s and became widespread in the 1800s. It is thought to have been popularised following P. T. Barnum's experience with an elephant named Toung Taloung that he billed as the 'Sacred White Elephant of Burma'. After much effort and great expense, Barnum finally acquired the animal from the King of Siam only to discover that his 'white elephant' was actually dirty grey in colour with a few pink spots.

"Crocodile Tears"

Meaning: Tears or expressions of sorrow that are insincere.

Origin: 'The Travels of Sir John Mandeville', written by the man himself 1357–71, collects his findings on his travels through Europe, Africa, The Far East and Arabia. In the book, it says that crocodiles shed tears while eating a man they captured.

Even though it is factually inaccurate, the phrase 'crocodile tears' found its way into Shakespeare's work and became an idiom in the sixteenth century, symbolising insincere grief in his play, 'Henry VI', (1591):

"The mournful crocodile that tricks its prey with sorrow."

"Break a Leg"

Meaning: Good luck.

Origin: Folklore throughout history has encouraged people to wish others bad luck since it was believed that wishing someone good luck would tempt evil spirits. In order to stop the evil spirits, people would wish bad luck as a way to not tempt fate. Other cultures believe the 'evil eye' watches those who receive too much praise and this dates back to at least 600 BC according to Greek texts. It is quite likely this belief has transferred through the ages and cultures.

'Break a leg' is most commonly said to actors and musicians before they go on stage to perform, and this is thought to date back to the 1920s. The first time it is seen in print in the 'good luck' manner is in Robert Wilson Lynd's 'A Defence of Superstition' (1921):

In horse racing, one would never wish someone good luck as it might push one's luck too far. You would say, rather, "I hope your horse will break a leg."

"Give the Cold Shoulder"

Meaning: Reject or be deliberately unfriendly to someone.

Origin: The first recorded use of the expression was by Sir Walter Scott in old Scots language, in 'The Antiquary' (1816) :

"Ye may mind that the Countess's dislike did na gang farther at first than just shewing o' the cauld shouther."

Experts believe the explanation of the expression is due to a very literal action, keeping one's back towards another person one was trying to avoid.

Despite being repeated in several books of etymology, the common explanation that the phrase stems from serving a cold shoulder of mutton or other meat to an unwanted guest is an incorrect folk etymology according to linguists.

"Kick the Bucket"

Meaning: To die.

Origin: There are two theories for this idiom. The first being, when killing a cow at slaughterhouses, people would place a bucket under the animal while it was positioned on a pulley. While trying to adjust the animal, the cow would kick out its legs and therefore kick the bucket before being killed.

The second theory, which has more evidence, is based on the removal of a bucket from someone killed by hanging. This shows its earliest appearance is in the 'Dictionary of the Vulgar Tongue' (1785), where it is defined as 'to die'. In John Badcock's slang dictionary of 1823, the explanation is given that:

"One Bolsover having hung himself from a beam while standing on a pail, or bucket, kicked this vessel away."

"Show Your True Colours"

Meaning: Reveal one's real character or intentions, especially when these are disreputable or dishonourable.

Origin: To confuse ones enemies, warships would use multiple flags. Warfare rules, however, dictated that ships must show their actual flag's 'true colours' before firing and hence the phrase.

The phrase itself dates back to at least the 1600s and can be seen as a metaphor in print from the mid-sixteenth century. The first printed example found is in Thomas Becon's 'A Fruitful Treatise of Fasting' (1551), in it he states the devil:

"Setteth forth him selfe in his true colours."

Shakespeare uses the phrase in 'Henry IV Pt 2' (1600):

"How might we see Falstaffe bestow himself to night in his true colours, and not our selues be seene?"

"Close but No Cigar"

Meaning: Almost but not quite successful.

Origin: At the end of the nineteenth century, fairgrounds and carnivals were very popular, particularly in the USA. At this time, the attractions were targeted at adults rather than children. The winners of games would quite often get a cigar as a prize, rather than the stuffed animals we see today. If the person was close to winning but did not succeed, they'd say it was 'close but no cigar'.

This is originally an American expression but is found used elsewhere too. The first recorded use of 'close but no cigar' in print is in Sayre and Twist's publishing of the script of the 1935 film version of 'Annie Oakley'.

"Waking Up on the Wrong Side of the Bed"

Meaning: Start the day in a bad temper.

Origin: This idiom is thought to have originated in ancient Rome. Romans were very careful always to get up on the correct side of the bed to ensure that good luck would follow them through their days. If they got up 'left foot forward' or 'on the wrong side of the bed', they believed that they would be unlucky.

Historically, since then, the left side of everything was considered to be 'the evil side'. So waking up on the left side was also considered a sign of bad luck. To ward off evil, people would push their beds to the left side of the room so they would have no other option than to get up on the right side of bed. The phrase itself 'getting up on the wrong side of bed' is first seen in the Oxford English Dictionary in 1801, but its origins are much older.

"Go Cold Turkey"

Meaning: To quit something abruptly.

Origin: The most common theory for this phrase is that during drug, tobacco, or alcohol withdrawal the skin of addicts can turn hard to the touch, covered with goosebumps and similar to the skin of a plucked turkey and this is thought to be the reason for this saying.

This is a very logical reason for the phrase and the expression first appeared in its full context in 'the Daily Colonist' in British Columbia in 1921: "Perhaps the most pitiful figures who have appeared before Dr Carleton Simon are those who voluntarily surrender themselves. When they go before him they are given what is called the 'cold turkey' treatment."

There is another theory of where the saying itself comes from however and the first reference to someone receiving 'cold turkey' in a negative context is in the UK magazine 'Judy' in 1877. In this magazine is a story of a guest who is given cold turkey instead of roasted with all the trimmings and is very upset with the meal presented to them.

"Put a Sock in It"

Meaning: Stop talking.

Origin: In the late nineteenth century, people used socks to stuff the horns of their gramophones or record players to lower the sound, since the machines had no volume controllers.

The earliest example of it in print that can be found, is a definition of the term in the weekly literary review 'The Athenaeum' (1919):

"The expression 'Put a sock in it', meaning 'Leave off talking, singing or shouting'."

Bert Thomas (1883–1966) created a poster for the British Ministry of Information during World War II, illustrating a soldier putting a sock in a gramophone to highlight the importance of being quiet and this may have brought the phrase to the fore.

"Son of a Gun"

Meaning: A jocular or affectionate way of addressing or referring to someone.

Origin: The phrase 'son of a gun' is thought to have originated in the British Royal Navy during the 1800s when sailors would sometimes take their wives on long ocean voyages. It is believed that if the woman gave birth on a ship, it should take place between the cannons on the ship's gun deck, since it was the most secluded place. Because of this reason, a child that was born on a ship would be called 'a son of a gun'. The first known printed example of 'son of a gun' is 'The British Apollo No. 43' (1708):

"You're a Son of a Gun."

"Best Man"

Meaning: A male friend or relative chosen by a bridegroom to assist him at his wedding.

Origin: It is said that during feudal times, it was possible that a rival Lord would try to break up a wedding ceremony and steal the bride for political reasons. To avoid any trouble, grooms would ask their best friends to stand next to them during the ceremony so they would help during the possible battle. The man, standing next to the groom was named 'Best Man'.

While the role is clearly older, the earliest printed use of the term 'best man' comes from 1782, observing that 'best man and best maid' in the Scottish dialect are equivalent to 'bride-man and bride-maid' in England.

"Steal One's Thunder"

Meaning: Win praise for oneself by pre-empting someone else's attempt to impress.

Origin: Playwright John Dennis (1657–1734) created a machine that could perfectly mimic the sound of thunder, by rattling a sheet of tin, for his play 'Appius and Virginia' (1709). His play wasn't a success, but somebody had taken note of his clever invention.

When, later on in another theatre, Dennis found somebody had copied his thunder machine when he was watching Macbeth and was using it without credit to him. He is quoted as saying,

"They will not let my play run but they steal my thunder."

"Get One's Goat"

Meaning: Irritate someone.

Origin: During horse racing, some horses would get anxious, so owners would place goats in the stalls with them to calm them down. Rival horse owners would sometimes steal these goats which would upset a horse and impact its chances of winning.

The phrase originated in the US, and the first entry found in print referring to its current meaning of someone being angry comes from a story about a burst water pipe that was printed in the US newspaper 'The Stevens Point Daily Journal', in May 1909:

"Wouldn't that get your goat? We'd been transferring the same water all night from the tub to the bowl and back again."

"Codswallop"

Meaning: Nonsense.

Origin: The most widely quoted story is that of Hiram Codd, an English soft drinks maker during the 1870s, who developed a technique for bottling lemonade. 'Wallop' is a slang term for beer, and beer drinkers would certainly be unhappy with bottled soft drinks. That being said, this is only theory.

It is not for nearly ninety years after, that the earliest reference is found in print as the title of a sketch by the Anglo-Australian artist Richard Larter, which he created in 1958, while still living in England.

'Load of Codswallop' gained more currency the following year, in the script of a 1959 episode of the popular UK television series 'Hancock's Half Hour'.

"Let the Cat Out of the Bag"

Meaning: Reveal a secret carelessly or by mistake.

Origin: Some time ago, farmers who sold pigs would bring them to the market wrapped up in a bag. Unscrupulous ones may have replaced the pig with a cat and if someone would accidentally let the cat out, their fraud would be uncovered.

There is no written evidence of this activity from the time, however, we do know pigs were bagged for sale and Richard Hill's 'Common-place Book' from 1530 offers some advice to merchants that led to another idiom:

"When ye proffer the pigge open the poke."

The first documented use of the phrase in its current meaning comes from a book review in a 1760 issue of 'The London Magazine':

"We could have wished that the author had not let the cat out of the bag."

"The Whole Nine Yards"

Meaning: To do everything that is possible or available.

Origin: The most popular theory is that during World War II, pilots would have a nine-yard chain of ammunition. When a fighter pilot used all of their ammunition on one target, they would give 'the whole nine yards'.

This may well be the case, but looking back earlier and we can see 'the whole six yards', was used in rural South America as early as 1912. That's still how the phrase goes in parts of the South, but it was inflated to 'nine yards' when it caught on elsewhere, the same way the early twentieth-century 'cloud seven' was upgraded to our 'cloud nine'.

The fact is that once you've said 'the whole' it doesn't matter what words you finish it with or whether they mean anything or not, 'the whole ball of wax' first showed up in the 1880s. There is no definitive origin, I will let you make up your own mind.

"Sleep Tight"

Meaning: Sleep well.

Origin: Popular theory is that the saying comes from Shakespeare's time when mattresses were secured by ropes. During that time, sleeping tight meant sleeping with the ropes pulled tight, making a well-sprung bed. This, however, cannot be the case.

Rope beds were invented in the sixteenth century and fell out of fashion quickly after the invention of the coil spring mattress in 1865. The first recorded use of the phrase 'sleep tight' wasn't until 1866 in Susan Bradford Eppes's journal entitled 'Through Some Eventful Years'. She writes on May 2:

"Goodbye, little diary. Sleep tight and wake bright."

Therefore, the late use of this phrase in comparison to the invention of rope beds signals that it must have some other origin.

According to the Oxford dictionary, the closely related adverb 'tightly' also meant 'safely' or 'soundly'. Put simply the saying comes from saying sleep safely.

"Pull Out All the Stops"

Meaning: Make a great effort to achieve something.

Origin: All evidence to the origin of 'Pull out all the stops', points to the construction of pipe organs. According to the American Guild of Organists:

"The pipes are arranged in rows or ranks, according to these tone colours. To bring a rank of pipes into play, the organist pulls a knob or operates a tablet called a 'stop'."

The first recorded use of the phrase in a figurative sense, was by Matthew Arnold, in 'Essays in Criticism' (1865), which reads:

"Knowing how unpopular a task one is undertaking when one tries to pull out a few more stops."

"Spill the Beans"

Meaning: Reveal secret information unintentionally or indiscreetly.

Origin: The common theory is that this saying comes from Ancient Greece, where voting was done using beans. Citizens would put a white bean into the jar of a candidate they support, and a black one for a candidate of whom they do not approve.

Though this is the most popular theory, there is no written evidence. What we can say is that since the sixteenth century, when used as a verb, 'spill' has also meant 'divulge' or 'let out'. One instance of this use of 'spill' in the 1500s is from Edward Hellowes' Guevara's Familiar Epistles. The passage reads:

"Although it be a shame to spill it, I will not leaue to say."

The earliest example of 'spill the beans' has been found in the United States from 'The Stevens Point Journal' from June 1908:

"He just walked off the reservation, taking enough insurgent Republicans with him to spill the beans for the big five."

We can say that the saying has been around for over 100 years in its current form, and find it likely that its origins lie in Ancient Greece.

"Run Amok"

Meaning: Behave uncontrollably and disruptively.

Origin: Amok, or running amok, is derived from the Malay word 'mengamok', which means to make a furious and desperate charge. Captain Cook is credited with making the first outside observations and recordings of amok in the Malay tribesmen in 1770 during his around-the-world voyage.

He described the affected individuals, who it is thought were under the influence of opium, as behaving violently without apparent cause and indiscriminately killing or maiming villagers and animals in a frenzied attack. Amok attacks involved an average of ten victims and ended when the individual was subdued or 'put down' by his fellow tribesmen, and frequently killed in the process.

According to Malay mythology, running amok was an involuntary behaviour caused by the 'hantu belian', or evil tiger spirit entering a person's body and compelling him or her to behave violently without conscious awareness. Because of their spiritual beliefs, those in the Malay culture tolerated running amok despite its devastating effects on the tribe.

"Hold a Candle To..."

Meaning: To be as good or desirable as someone or something.

Origin: This phrase originates from when apprentices were expected to hold the candle up, so their more experienced colleagues could see what they were doing. The phrase first appeared in print in Sir Edward Dering's 'The Fower Cardinal-Vertues of a Carmelite Fryar', 1641: "Though I be not worthy to hold the candle to Aristotle."

"Resting on One's Laurels"

Meaning: Be so satisfied with what one has already achieved that one makes no further effort.

Origin: Although we cannot trace the saying back this far, we do know that to the Ancient Greeks, laurel branches symbolised victory and success. This is closely tied to Apollo, the god of music, prophecy and poetry. Laurel branches were given to victorious athletes in ancient Greece and later to Generals who won important battles, thus the term 'laureates' and the later phrase 'resting on laurels'.

We can trace the use of laurels back to at least 200 BC through Ancient Greek coins that have been found with images of Apollo wearing laurels.

Not until the nineteenth century did the term receive a negative connotation to describe those who are overly satisfied with their achievements. The first example found with this change of Laurels can be seen in Emanuel Deutsch's 'Literary Remains' (1874):

"Let them rest on their Laurels for a while."

"Eat Humble Pie"

Meaning: Make a humble apology and accept humiliation.

Origin: In the Middle Ages, there would be a huge feast after a hunt. The Lord of the manor would receive the finest piece of meat, and the ones with a lower status would eat a pie filled with entrails and innards, which were also known as 'umbles', 'numbles' or 'humbles'. Those who would eat the 'umble pie' were considered to be humiliated, since it symbolised their lower status.

According to the Merriam-Webster 'New Book of Word Histories', humble pie was recorded from before 1642, and that there were variations to the name through time – 'numbles' by the 1300s, which by the 1400s became 'umbles', which became 'humbles' by the 1500s.

"Hands Down"

Meaning: Easily and decisively.

Origin: Hands down is an idiom from the world of horse racing and is a rather logical one. The jockey is so far ahead of the chasing pack that they can sit back and relax, they can win the race without even holding the reigns.

There are numerous examples found in print from 1830 onwards. At this point, the expression was literal, an example being 'Independence won with hands down'.

The first example in print of the metaphorical meaning can be found in the 'London Evening Herald' newspaper in 1861:

"Soon after rounding the turn into the straight, Marignan deprived Bannerdale of the lead, and won hands down by four lengths, half a length between the second and third."

"Take the P**s"

Meaning: To mock someone or something.

Origin: There are numerous 'origins' for this, the most popular theory harks back to when clothes were dyed with natural dye. Stale urine was used as a mordant, which stops the natural dye from leaching out of the cloth.

The textile industry needed all the urine it could get, so workers would go around and collect specially designated chamber pots full of urine from people's houses. It was the least desirable job at the time, so people who did it would often lie about their profession. There is no evidence to support this theory in print however.

The other main and possibly more likely origin is from the word micturition, the medical term for urinating, which would lead to 'taking the mickey' or alternatively 'take the p**s' but we cannot be certain. The only certainty, wherever the origin lies is that the saying has been seen in print from the 1930s. The saying is likely to be much more recent than the stories it refers to.

"Read the Riot Act"

Meaning: Give someone a strong warning that they must improve their behaviour.

Origin: The term 'read the riot act' has its origins in an actual law called the 'Riot Act' which was enacted in Britain in 1714. 'The Riot Act' was a legal document, that was read aloud in front of a crowd bigger than 12 people that were considered a threat to the peace.

A public official would read a small part of the Act and order people to leave peacefully within an hour, anyone that remained after one hour was subject to arrest or removal by force.

"Happy as Larry"

Meaning: Someone who is very happy.

Origin: The 'Larry' in question here is thought to be Australian middleweight boxer, Larry Foley (1847–1917). He retired undefeated at the age of 32, in the 1870s. He is thought to have garnered prize money of $150,000 dollars, which was an incredible amount of money at the time.

All the early examples in print are of Australian or New Zealand origin which fits well. The earliest printed reference is from the New Zealand writer G.L. Meredith in 1875:

"We would be as happy as Larry if it were not for the rats."

"Thick as Thieves"

Meaning: Intimate or closely allied.

Origin: This idiom is believed to originate in the seventeenth century but the phrase is not seen in print until the nineteenth. At that time, thieves would work together in gangs and were extremely close, telling each other everything and would rely on each other. 'Thick' in this case means 'very close' or 'closely packed'.

Thieves were established as being 'thick' by the late seventeenth century. It is surprising that 'as thick as thieves' didn't emerge until a century or so later. The records of the Old Bailey, which list transcripts of cases held there since 1674 and which might be just the place to find this phrase, doesn't list it until 1874.

The first example found of it in print is from the English newspaper The Morning Chronicle, in a letter dated March 1827, published in February 1828:

"Bill Morris and me are as thick as two thieves."

"Paint the Town Red"

Meaning: Go out and enjoy oneself flamboyantly.

Origin: There are two versions on how this idiom came into use. First, it is believed that back in 1837 a famous mischief maker known as the 'Marquis of Waterford' had a wild night out with his group of friends, during which they knocked over flowerpots, pulled knockers off doors and even broke windows. One of their biggest acts of vandalism was painting the doors of several homes with red paint.

The other version of the story says that the origin of this idiom might have originated from the brothels of the American West, where they referred to drunk men behaving as if the whole town was a red-light district.

The first example of the phrase in print is seen in 'The New York Times' in 1883:

"Then the Democrats charged upon the street cars, and being wafted into Newark proceeded, to use their own metaphor, to 'paint the town red'."

"Beat About the Bush"

Meaning: Discuss a matter without coming to the point.

Origin: Beating about the bush was an action performed while hunting in medieval times, the action of actually hitting the area surrounding bushes to drive birds and other animals out into the open. After this was done, others would then catch the animals.

The earliest version of this found in print is in a medieval poem *Generydes – A Romance in Seven Line Stanzas* (1440):

"Butt as it hath be sayde full long agoo, some bete the bussh and some the byrdes take."

"Ice Breaker" or "Break the Ice"

Meaning: Do or say something to relieve tension or get conversation going in a strained situation or when strangers meet.

Origin: In the 1800s, commercial ships would often get stuck in frozen waters during winter time, so smaller ships called 'icebreakers' would come to clear a path to shore by breaking the ice. This is the most common theory for where the saying comes from however, the phrase was already in use by this point and it is likely these ships just popularised the saying.

The first recorded version is actually 200 years prior from Sir Thomas North in his 1579 translation of Plutarch's 'Lives of the Noble Grecians and Romanes':

"To be the first to break the Ice of the Enterprise," and was thought to mean to forge a path for others to follow.

The first time we see the saying in its current form, to create relaxation in an awkward situation, is in Samuel Butler's 'Hudibras' (1664):

"The Orator – At last broke silence, and the Ice."

"Show a Leg"

Meaning: Get out of bed; get up.

Origin: Just before ships were about to leave port, sailors would try to sneak in a lady and hide them in their hammock. Before leaving, officers would ask anyone in a hammock to 'show a leg.' If a hairless leg appeared, the woman was asked to leave the ship quickly.

It is first recorded in print, with the form 'shew', in 'Travels of Four Years and a Half in the United States of America' (1798– 1803), by the British author John Davies (1774–1854):

"Heave out there! Heave out! Shew a leg there! Shew a leg! Must I send a hauling-line down for you starbaulins?"

"More Than You Can Shake a Stick At"

Meaning: A large amount or quantity of something.

Origin: The common theory for this idiom is that farmers, who waved sticks to herd sheep, would have more sheep than they could control. The earliest examples in script don't back up this theory, although presumably, by the time it is put in print the phrase is already well known.

The other main theory is that the stick in question may well have been a sword or other weapon and that there were too many to handle with the 'stick' but again there is no evidence to back this theory either.

What we can say for sure is that the phrase is at least 200 years old with the first example of it being used in its current format according to the Oxford English Dictionary in the issue of the 'Lancaster Journal of Pennsylvania' dated 5 August 1818:

"We have in Lancaster as many Taverns as you can shake a stick at."

"Has a Nice Ring to It"

Meaning: Something that sounds pleasant.

Origin: When testing the quality of an anvil, a blacksmith will strike it with a hammer to see how well it bounces back. A good quality anvil will have good bounce back, and the noise of the blow will produce a painful ringing sensation in your ears, hence 'has a nice ring to it'.

"Pleased as Punch"

Meaning: Feeling great delight or pride.

Origin: This phrase is derived from the Punch and Judy puppet shows that were popular from 1660 in the United Kingdom; the shows are still being shown to this day.

Punch was the villain and main character of the show and killed people, taking great pleasure in doing so, from which the saying 'pleased as Punch' and 'Proud as Punch' was born. Punch also created another popular phrase that has been used by many others since – "That's the way to do it."

The saying was used many times over the centuries and was even used in Charles Dickens 'Hard times', 1854: *"When Sissy got into the school, her father was pleased as punch."*

"Don't Throw the Baby Out with the Bathwater"

Meaning: Discard something valuable along with other things that are undesirable.

Origin: 'Throw the baby out with the bathwater' was originally a German saying and the earliest printed reference can be seen in Thomas Murner's satirical work 'Narrenbeschwörung' (1512):

"Schüttet das Kind mit dem Bade aus," meaning exactly the same as the later English version of the phrase.

Scottish philosopher, Thomas Carlyle, was well acquainted with German proverbs and translated it in an essay in 1849 :

"You must empty-out the bathing-tub, but not the baby along with it."

The popular theory is that in the sixteenth century, most people would bathe very infrequently and in the same bath tub, men of the house would bathe first, followed by females and finally children. At the end of this routine, the water would be so dirty and cloudy that mothers would have to be careful not to throw their infants out with the water. This, however, is only a theory and is not backed up by any fact or any incident in print of this ever actually happening.

"No Spring Chicken"

Meaning: Someone who is no longer young, past his prime.

Origin: The origin of the phrase comes from an earlier phrase 'Now past a chicken' meaning no longer young. This phrase is first recorded in print in 1711 in a book by Steele, 'The Spectator':

"You ought to consider you are now past a chicken."

'No spring chicken' is an intensified version of the phrase and can first be seen in print first in 1906 according to Robert Hendrickson in 'Encyclopaedia of Word and Phrase Origins'.

The common theory is that farmers found chickens born in the spring brought better prices than 'old' ones that had gone through the winter. Farmers who tried to sell the old birds as 'new spring born' would have complaints that they were 'no spring chicken'. Over time, this phrase has come to be used figuratively for anything that was seen as past its prime.

"By and Large"

Meaning: On the whole; everything considered.

Origin: This phrase is usually used as a synonym for 'all things considered' and originates in the sixteenth century, where the word 'large' meant that a ship was sailing with the wind at its back and the word 'by' meant the opposite, that the ship was sailing into the wind.

The mariners used the phrase 'by and large' to refer quite simply to sailing in any and all directions, relative to the wind.

The earliest printed reference to this saying is from Samuel Sturmy in 'The Mariners Magazine' (1669):

"Thus you see the ship handled in fair weather and foul, by and large."

We do, however, see the individual words 'By and Large' being used individually in reference to the direction of the wind the century before.

"Jaywalker"

Meaning: One who crosses or walks in the street or road unlawfully or without regard for approaching traffic.

Origin: The word 'jaywalk' is a word derived from the words 'jay', meaning an inexperienced person and a derisory word that originated in the early 1900s, and 'walk'.

While jaywalking is associated with pedestrians today, the earliest references to 'jay' behaviour in the road were about horse-drawn carriages and automobiles in the very early twentieth century as in 'jay drivers' who did not drive on the right side of the street.

The term swiftly expanded to pedestrians, and by 1909, 'The Chanute Daily Tribune' warned:

"The jay walker needs attention as well as the jay driver."

The earliest citation in the Oxford English Dictionary follows in 1917. Automobile interests in the US took up the cause of labelling and scorning jaywalkers in the 1910s and early 1920s, by then the earlier term of 'jay driver' was declining in use.

Why the word 'Jay'? There is no definitive proof but the thought is that it derives from the word 'joy' as in 'joy rider'.

"Catch My Drift"

Meaning: Do you understand me?

Origin: One of the common theories is that this saying has something to do with drift wood but that is not the case.

According to the 'Oxford English Dictionary', 'drift' meaning the sense of 'what one is getting at' is from 1520s. The earliest example of drift in this format being 1526:

"Harde it is, to perceyue the processe and dryfte of this treatyse."

Catch, as in the noun meaning 'that which is caught or worth catching' is from 1596.

The phrase 'catch my drift' in its current form, however, does not appear until 1969 in the 'American Heritage Dictionary'. There is no definitive answer as to where the phrase comes from in its current form, but the above individual breakdown of the two words might be an indicator.

"By Hook or by Crook"

Meaning: By any means necessary.

Origin: This saying has no definitive origin, but the most likely one derives from the custom in medieval England of allowing peasants to take from royal forests whatever deadwood they could pull down with a shepherd's crook or cut with a reaper's bill-hook.

This feudal custom was recorded in the 1820s by the English rural campaigner William Cobbett, although the custom itself long pre-dates that reference.

Although there are multiple potential origins of this saying, it can actually be traced all the way back to 1390 in John Gowers 'Confessio Amantis':

"What with hepe and what with croke they make her maister ofte winne."

Hepe was the medieval name for a curved hook and croke meant perjury.

"Gardening Leave"

Meaning: An employee when leaving a job is instructed to stay away from work during the notice period, while still remaining on the payroll.

Origin: The term originated in the British Civil Service, where employees had the right to request special leave for exceptional purposes. The term is believed to have come from employers stating the employee when not in the office was allowed to work in their own home and look after their garden. The term came to more widespread public attention in 1986 where it was used in the BBC sitcom 'Yes, Prime Minister' episode, 'One of Us'.

"Wild Goose Chase"

Meaning: Pursuing something that seems to be pointless.

Origin: This phrase's origin is believed to be based on sixteenth-century horse racing. A 'wild goose chase' was a horse race in which the lead rider would be chased by other riders. It was said to be similar to how geese flying in a formation and follow the leader.

We can see the phrase itself was being used commonly by 1592, as Shakespeare uses it in 'Romeo and Juliet':

"Nay, if thy wits run the wild-goose chase, I have done, for thou hast more of the wild-goose in one of thy wits than, I am sure, I have in my whole five."

"One-Trick Pony"

Meaning: Limited to only one single talent.

Origin: The idiom one-trick pony is thought to derive from the circus. A circus featuring a pony that has can only perform one trick would not be very entertaining. An old joke claims that a certain circus was so bad; the one trick the pony performed was to play dead.

The term 'one trick pony' to describe a circus horse act featuring an animal with a small repertoire of talents first appeared around the turn of the twentieth century. The first example found is in 'Transactions of the Oregon Pioneer Association' (1898):

"The marvels that were seen at the first one-tent were one-clown and one-trick-pony."

By the mid-twentieth century, the term 'one trick pony' was expanded to anything that does just one thing and started to be used as an idiom.

"Clever Clogs"

Meaning: an intellectual who is all too keen to flaunt his intelligence to the point of being irritating.

Origin: 'Clever boots' is thought to be the original saying and 'Boots' was a sixteenth- and seventeenth- century term for the common man, meaning anybody. We still see 'Boots' being used in terms such as 'Bossy boots' and 'clever boots' is still used but mainly seen in Australia.

Why did it change to clogs? It is thought most likely it became 'clogs' due to the 'cl' alliteration used like 'silly billy' or 'okey dokey'.

"Gordon Bennett"

Meaning: Unbelievable or an expression of surprise.

Origin: This expression is primarily used in the UK, even though the father of the Gordon Bennett in question made his name in the US. James Gordon Bennett senior (1795–1872) was a Scottish-born journalist, famous in the US for founding the New York Herald and conducting the first ever newspaper interview.

Gordon Bennett junior (1841–1918), was something of an international playboy. He was as 'a dandy' and was known for his wild ways and outrageous parties. Gordon junior used his inheritance to sponsor the Bennett Trophy in motor racing from 1900 to 1905, and in 1906 established a hot-air balloon race that is still held today.

"Having a Field Day"

Meaning: Extract excitement or gain an advantage from a situation.

Origin: Field day was a military term used in the 1700s that referred to a day dedicated to military manoeuvres outdoors, or 'in the field', as early tactics dictated that opposing armies met on vast fields (hence the term 'battlefield').

The first time we see this in print is in the London newspaper 'The Daily Journal' in1723:

"Yesterday was Field Day for the Horse in Hide-Park, when one of the four Troops of Guards passed in Review there before the several Officers of their own Corps."

The term can be seen in this way throughout the 1800s and by the 1900s, the term field day came to mean any day during which exciting or big events occurred as they would often happen in fields. The earliest example seen where not related to military activity can be seen in journals by Lord Byron in 1823:

"Sometimes a dance, though rarely on field days. For then the gentlemen were rather tired."

"Mexican Standoff"

Meaning: A stalemate or impasse.

Origin: In Mexico, these standoffs were common among the bandits, Vaqueros, charros, chinacos and pistoleros. It was a way of settling a problem amongst two or more people.

Furthermore, it was a matter of pride, proving their masculinity by demonstrating that victory could be achieved without backstabbing, cheating or cowardice. This was a fair way that granted both parties the opportunity to stand face-to-face and gamble their life by relying on their speed and agility as well as accuracy with their gun.

The first time this phrase is seen in print is in the 'New York Sunday Mercury' in 1876, in a short story by F. Harvey Smith about an American being held up by a Mexican bandit, and the outcome:

"Go," he said sternly then. "We will call it a stand-off, a Mexican stand-off, you lose your money, but you save your life!"

"Don't Know You from Adam"

Meaning: Someone you would not know if you met them.

Origin: Used since the 1800s, this idiom derives from the biblical story of Adam, the first man, created by God. The idea seems to be that Adam lived so long ago that nobody living today could possibly recognise him. Charles Dickens uses the expression in his story The Old Curiosity Shop, 1840:

"He called to see my Governor this morning," replied Mr Chuckster, "beyond that, I don't know him from Adam."

"Murphy's Law" and "Sod's Law"

Meaning: Anything that can go wrong will go wrong.

Origin: The term Murphy's Law was coined in the early 1950s during G-force tests by the American Air Force.

The story goes that an aerospace engineer named Captain Edward A. Murphy installed a key sensor backwards, skewing the test results. Another version of the story states that Captain Murphy did no such thing, that the reason he is associated with Murphy's Law is that he frequently expressed the idea that anything that can go wrong will go wrong. Eventually, other members of the team began to refer to this sentiment as Murphy's Law.

Sod's Law is a British axiom that is somewhat similar to Murphy's Law, but with a twist. Sod's Law carries a sense of being mocked by fate. Sod's Law is related to the idea of the unlucky sod, an average person who has bad luck. Sod's Law first appears in the 1970s.

"Bob's Your Uncle"

Meaning: A way to express the ease with which a task can be achieved.

Origin: The most common theory is that the expression arose after Conservative Prime Minister Robert Gascoyne-Cecil, 3rd Marquess of Salisbury. 'Bob', as he was known, appointed his nephew Arthur Balfour as Chief Secretary for Ireland in 1887, an act of nepotism, which was apparently both surprising and unpopular. The saying is thought to have become more popular following the release of a song by Florrie Forde in 1931 with the lyrics :

"Bob's your uncle, follow your uncle Bob, he knows what to do, he'll look after you."

"For Pete's Sake"

Meaning: An expression of frustration or feeling exasperated.

Origin: 'For Pete's sake' originated as a substitute for 'for Christ's sake', and other similar expressions. Some people believe one of Jesus's disciples, St Peter, is the 'Pete' here although there is no written evidence of this. 'For Pete's sake' is a less blasphemous way of expressing Jesus Christ's name in vain. Other examples are 'For heaven's sake' and 'for pity's sake'.

According to the Oxford English Dictionary, ' Pete's sake' came into use more than a century ago and prompted similar sayings such as 'for the love of Pete' in 1906 and 'in the name of Pete' in 1942 so the use of 'Pete' may be based on ancient characters but is not an ancient saying.

"Keep a Stiff Upper Lip"

Meaning: Show courage in the face of pain or adversity.

Origin: The phrase 'keep a stiff upper lip' refers to holding one's face in an unemotional, deadpan fashion so as not to betray emotions such as fear, distaste, revulsion, sorrow, etc. The ideal of the stiff upper lip is thought to be traced back to Ancient Greece, to the Spartans, whose cult of discipline and self-sacrifice was a source of inspiration to the English public school system.

The expression' keep a stiff upper lip' was popularised by the novel 'Stiff Upper Lip, Jeeves' by P.G. Wodehouse and published in 1963. Interestingly, the idiom 'keep a stiff upper lip' originated as an American way to describe staying resolute without giving way to emotion. In time, Americans came to use the term to describe Englishmen.

"It Ain't Over 'Til the Fat Lady Sings"

Meaning: It's not over until the end.

Origin: The most commonly thought of origin is a musical connection with the familiar operatic role of Brunnhilde in Richard Wagner's 'Götterdämmerung', the last of the immensely long, four-opera Ring Cycle. Brunnhilde is usually depicted as a well-upholstered lady who appears for a ten minute solo to conclude proceedings.

This saying is also used in sporting events and is first attributed to sportswriter and broadcaster Dan Cook, who used the phrase after the first basketball game between the San Antonio Spurs and the Washington Wizards, then called the Washington Bullets, during the 1978 NBA Playoffs.

"Taking the Mickey"

Meaning: To ridicule or be ridiculed.

Origin: Also known as 'Taking the Michael' or 'Taking the Mick'. 'Take the Mickey' is thought to be an abbreviated form of the Cockney rhyming slang 'take the Mickey Bliss', a euphemism for 'take the p**s'. It has also been suggested that 'mickey' is a contraction of 'micturition' which is the medical name for the act of urinating. In which case, 'take the micturition' would be a synonymous euphemism for 'take the p**s'. Whichever is the case the phrase has been noted since the 1930s.

"Bloody Nora"

Meaning: Surprised or shocked.

Origin: There are a few theories on this one but the most common is that Bloody Norah was originally just called Norah and was the maid for the wealthy Duke Wodingtonshire in the seventeenth century. She earned the name Bloody Norah after she killed a servant of the duke.

When the duke caught her repeatedly slapping the bloody corpse with a stick of celery he shouted, "Oh dear god you're all bloody, Norah," and after beating her he banished her to a basement cell for three years.

This has absolutely no evidence to back it up in print anywhere and the Duke Wodingtonshire can't be found in any records. The truth is this one may well have been lost in the sands of time but this fanciful story is the most popular.

"Hat-Trick"

Meaning: Three successes of the same kind within a limited time period.

Origin. Though commonly used in reference to soccer or ice hockey, the term actually first appeared in 1858 in cricket, to describe H. H. Stephenson's taking three wickets with three consecutive deliveries. Fans held a collection for Stephenson, and presented him with a hat bought with the proceeds. The term was used in print for the first time in 1865 in the Chelmsford Chronicle:

"With his second ball bowled the Romford leviathan, Mr Beauchamp, and afterwards performed the hat trick by getting three wickets in the over."

"Swinging the Lead"

Meaning: Shirking one's duties or being lazy.

Origin: Before the days of sonar, ships would determine the depth of the water by posting a sailor at the front of the ship with a lead weight attached to a long rope. Therefore, a sailor who was swinging the lead and not actually dropping and retrieving it, which was an arduous task, was being lazy. At this point, it was known as 'heaving the lead'.

The phrase in its current guise, however, isn't first recorded until 1917 during WWI, the magazine 'Today' published this:

"It is evident that he had 'swung the lead' until he got his discharge."

"At the End of One's Tether"

Meaning: A state in which one is not able to deal with a problem or difficult situation.

Origin: A tether is a rope or chain tied to an animal to restrict its movement. The term at the end of one's tether is primarily a British phrase, from the Old Swedish word, *tiuther*. The idea is of an animal that has been tethered and left to graze and runs out of length.

The first printed versions of the saying can be seen in Sir John Chardin's 'The coronation of Solyman' (1686):

"Being run to the end of his rope."

The earliest version of 'The end of my tether' can be seen in the comedy play 'The Contrast' (1787).

"Start from Scratch"

Meaning: to begin again.

Origin: The 'scratch' originally referred to the starting line of a race or sporting line of some sort 'scratched' into the ground, from which all runners or players would be starting without a head start.

The first time that such a 'scratch' is referred to in print is in a cricketing manual – John Nyren's Young Cricketer's Tutor, 1833, which records this line from a 1778 work by Cotton:

"Ye strikers, Stand firm to your scratch, let your bat be upright."

"Step Up to the Plate"

Meaning: Take action in response to an opportunity or crisis.

Origin: The idiom is derived from the American sport of baseball. Home plate is the beginning position in baseball, designated by a flat marker known as home plate. The batter literally steps up to the plate in a designated area in order to swing at the pitched ball.

The first example found comes from the Illinois newspaper The Chicago Tribune, May 1874, in a game between the White Stockings and Hartford:

"The visitors were put out as fast as they stepped up to the plate."

"The Whole Kit and Kaboodle"

Meaning: 'Everything' or 'all of it'.

Origin: A kit is set of objects, as in a toolkit, or what a soldier would put in his kit-bag. A caboodle, or boodle, is an archaic term meaning group or collection, usually of people. There are several phrases similar to the whole kit and caboodle, which is first recorded in that form in 1884.

Most of them are of US origin and all the early citations are American. Caboodle was never in common use outside the USA and now has died out everywhere, apart from its use in this phrase.

"Not On Your Nelly"

Meaning: An emphatic form of 'no'.

Origin: This, apparently, is Cockney rhyming slang for 'not on your life' or 'not bloody likely'. The slang goes this way: Nelly rhymes with smelly, which leads to smelly breath, breath leads to breathing to keep alive, leading to 'not on your life'. The term can be found as far back as the 1930s in the UK.

"Back to Square One"

Meaning: Start again.

Origin: This originates from the days when football was listened to a lot on the radio. To help the listener picture the scene, the pitch was divided up into a grid of imaginary squares, square one being around the goal mouth. Early examples can be found in the radio times in 1927.

"Dead Ringer"

Meaning: An exact duplicate.

Origin: The expression 'dead ringer' comes from American horse racing and originated at the end of the nineteenth century, when a horse that would be raced under a false name and pedigree was called a ringer. The word 'dead' in this expression refers not to lifelessness, but to 'precise' or 'exact'.

"Pulling Your Leg"

Meaning: To trick or lie to someone in a playful way.

Origin: There is no definitive answer. However, the two most common theories are as follows.

Firstly, that thieves used to pull at people's legs to trip them and then use the disorientation as an opportunity to rob them. This was supposed to have taken place in 'Victorian London'.

The second theory is this, until 1783 Tyburn, London was the principal place of execution in England. Many notables were hanged there, including Oliver Cromwell, although he was blissfully unconcerned about it as he had spent the previous three years buried in Westminster Abbey and had to be exhumed in order to attend. The 'pulling my leg' theory is that people, the so called 'hangers on', were hired at Tyburn executions to hang onto the victim's legs in order to give them a quick end.

"Tongue in Cheek"

Meaning: In an ironic, flippant or insincere way.

Origin: This phrase first appears in print 1828 in The Fair Maid of Perth by Sir Walter Scott:

"The fellow who gave this all-hail thrust his tongue in his cheek to some scapegraces like himself."

It's not certain if Sir Walter Scott was using it in the ironic context we see today as in the idea of suppressed mirth, biting one's tongue to prevent an outburst of laughter. Another example of this would be to take things 'with a pinch of salt', which we will cover in another origin story.

There is no question that it is being used in this context just a few years later though in Richard Barham's 'The Ingoldsby Legends' (1845):

As he sarcastically says, "He cried 'Superb, Magnifique', with his tongue in his cheek."

"The Bee's Knees"

Meaning: A highly admired person or thing.

Origin: There are numerous theories with this particular one. However, the most popular is a reference to the fact that bees carry pollen in sacks on their knees, although bees have six leg sections, and that the expression therefore alludes to this concentrated goodness. This one might be open to some debate though.

'Bee's knees' began to be used in early twentieth-century America and there are several examples of it. The first example of it I can find in print, however, is actually in a New Zealand newspaper The West Coast Times in August 1906, which listed the cargo carried by the SS Zealandia as: ' A quantity of post holes, three bags of treacle and seven cases of bees' knees'.

The term shortly after seemed to spread quite quickly around the English-speaking world.

"Not a Cat in Hell's Chance"

Meaning: To be absolutely unable to achieve something.
Origin: This is a shortening of the more explicit saying:

"I have no more chance in life than a cat without claws."

This longer phrase is more logical than the shortened version which is more common today. The earliest instance of this phrase found is from Jackson's Oxford Journal of 29 September 1753.

"Saved My Bacon"

Meaning: To escape from injury or avoid harm.
Origin: By bacon, we now normally mean the cured and dried meat taken from the back or sides of a pig. To the medieval mind, 'bacon' was meat from anywhere on the body of the animal, more like what we now call pork.
This was the origin of the slang term 'bacon' meaning the human body. 'Saving your bacon' was simply saving your body from harm. The expression was used that way as early as the seventeenth century. The earliest version found is in Ireland's Momus Elenticus, 1654:

"Some fellowes there were, to save their bacon penn'd many a smooth song."

"Everything but the Kitchen Sink"

Meaning: Everything imaginable.

Origin: The phrase originated around the early 1900s and the first printed reference can be found in 1918 in the New York newspaper 'The Syracuse Herald'. The expression became popular during World War II, where it was said that everything but the kitchen sink was thrown at the enemy.

Another variant of the phrase, 'everything but the kitchen stove' predates this phrase and can be found in 1894 in the Jeffersonville National Democrat.

"Burn the Midnight Oil"

Meaning: Stay up late working or studying.

Origin: The origin of the phrase 'burn the midnight oil' dates back to pre-electric times when people mostly used oil lamps for lighting. The first written use of the term 'burn the midnight oil' is found in Quarles' Emblems, written in 1634. The reason, however, that the idiom refers primarily to work done by lamplight rather than leisure activities is based in a concept that predates oil lamps.

Back in the day, there was a verb in English which meant to work late by candlelight, 'elucubrate'. It has obviously passed out of common usage now but can be found in sources such as Henry Cockeram's 1623 English Dictionary:

"Elucubrate, to doe a thing by candlelight."

"Pig in a Poke"

Meaning: An offer or deal that is foolishly accepted.

Origin: The expression 'pig in a poke' is thought to come from the 1500s, where a 'poke' was a sack, and merchants would sell piglets in pokes, often unseen before purchase. When an unsuspecting buyer got his poke home and went to release the piglet, a chicken, duck, goose or some other animal less valuable than a pig would come out of the bundle instead.

The advice being given is 'don't buy anything until you have seen it'. The earliest recording in print is seen in Richard Hilles Common-place Book, 1530, which gave this advice to market traders:

"When ye proffer the pigge open the poke."

"The Dog's Boll**ks"

Meaning: The very best.

Origin: There are numerous theories for this one but the most common and my favourite theory is that the children's toy set Meccano, many years ago, came in two standards, Box Standard and Box Deluxe. Box Standard was the basic model and is believed to be the derivation of the term bog standard, which means average. Box Deluxe, on the other hand, was used by the workers in the Meccano factory to mean posh or high quality. Over time, Box Deluxe morphed into Dog's Boll**ks as workers swapped the initial letters of the words. It spread quickly and other versions, such as 'the mutt's nuts', 'the dog's danglies' and 'the poodle's privates' emerged soon afterwards.

"The Life of Riley"

Meaning: An easy life.

Origin: Some believe this saying originates in a popular song of the 1880s, 'Is That Mr Reilly?' by Pat Rooney, which later inspired a novel and 1920 silent film. The song described what its hero would do if he suddenly came into a fortune.

The question is whether this is where the term came from, whether this song was inspired by other events or was it just that the song was by chance relevant as the name 'Reilly' was a very common one at the time.

The first time we see it used in the context we use it in now can be found in print in New Jersey newspaper 'The News' in 1910:

"Henry Mungersdorf is living the life of Riley just at present."

If we look back slightly further, we can see in the 'Dublin Weekly Nation' newspaper in 1899 that a Mr Reiley was the hero of a popular folk ballad, living exactly the life that would lead to the coining of the phrase we have been seeking, here is an excerpt from the ballad:

"Oh rise up, Wiley Reilly, and come along with me, I mean to go with you and leave this country, to leave my father's dwelling, his houses and free land."

So, whilst we cannot be absolutely certain, it is thought the saying has been popularised by all the above and for certain the term has been used in one form or another as far back as 1880.

"Go Like the Clappers"

Meaning: To move extremely fast.

Origin: This idiom almost certainly comes from the times when all important news was spread to the local village or town by use of the church bells. The 'clappers' in question are the things that clang on the inside of the bell making the ringing sound. A vigorously rung bell implied a sense of urgency or speed. For example, 'The Norfolk News' in England in 1861 reported that, during a trial:

"For full twenty minutes, the tongues of the plaintiff and defendant went like the clappers of a couple of bells ."

That being said, although these bells were 'clappers' and were used at the time the idiom itself is not in print in its current meaning until as late as 1942 in a newspaper piece by Associated News staff Writer Alfred Wall, in which he listed various RAF slang terms:

A pilot chased by the enemy goes like the clappers, or full out.

"Three Sheets to the Wind"

Meaning: Very drunk.

Origin: In the days of sailing ships, the sails had ropes called 'sheets' at each corner, four for a square sail. These were used to trim the sail so that it caught the wind to best advantage. If one or more of the sheets was allowed to flap loose, the sail would get steadily harder to control, so if three out of four were flapping in the breeze the least change in the wind would catch it 'flat a-back' and probably split it.

It is easy to see how an out-of-control sail could be seen as an analogy of an out of control or drunk person. The phrase is these days, more often given as 'three sheets to the wind', rather than the original 'three sheets in the wind'. The earliest printed citation found is in Pierce Egan's Real life in London', 1821:

"Old Wax and Bristles is about three sheets in the wind."

"Windfall"

Meaning: An unexpected, unearned or sudden gain or advantage.

Origin: In feudal times, peasants weren't allowed to chop down the land owners trees for wood or fruit, but could collect anything that lay on the ground already. When there was a storm or strong winds, the peasants knew there would be an unexpected 'windfall' of good quality wood. This can be found in print as early as the 1540s.

In more modern times, the word has come to mean unexpected financial gain.

"Showing One's Mettle"

Meaning: Withstanding pressure or being resilient.

Origin: Metal was known as the hardest material and therefore showing one's mettle was showing how tough someone was. The phrase first appears in seventeenth-century texts. Back in the thirteenth century, 'metal' and 'mettle' were used interchangeably.

Over the centuries, the word 'mettle' lost its direct association with the cold, hard, solid material and by the eighteenth century, had become a figurative term describing one's personal constitution. The connotation of outer strength derived from the word 'metal' had simply been exchanged with the idea of human inner strength.

The first example of showing a strong constitution in the use of this term can be seen in John Fletcher's 'Monsieur Thomas', 1619: "What things done that shews a man and mettle?"

"Willy Nilly"

Meaning: Haphazardly or not caring.

Origin: Although we more commonly use this phrase nowadays to mean 'haphazardly', the origin centres around the first meaning. The early meaning of the word 'nill' was the opposite of 'will', as in 'wanting to do something'. In other words, 'nill' meant 'wanting to avoid doing something'. So, combining the two words – I am willing, I am unwilling – expresses the idea that it doesn't matter to me one way or the other.

The phrase dates back at least a millennium, with the earliest known version being the Old English text, Aelfric's 'Lives of Saints' circa 1000:

"Forean the we synd synfulle and sceolan beon eadmode, wille we, nelle we."

"Great Scott"

Meaning: Expressing surprise or amazement.

Origin: The reference is to General Winfield Scott (1786 – 1866), who commanded one of the two American armies in the Mexican War (1846 to 1848) and was the Union General-in-Chief at the beginning of the Civil War. Scott stood 6'5" and is said to have weighed as much as 300 pounds by the end of his life.

"What a monster size he was!" Virginia congressman John Sergeant Wise wrote in 1899. "His talk was like the roaring of a lion, his walk like the tread of the elephant."

This and other evidence, although not conclusive, points strongly to Winfield Scott as the source of 'Great Scott'!

"Carrots Help You See in the Dark"

Meaning: Carrots help improve one's night vision.

Origin: This originated in WW2. The British invented radar which helped our pilots pick up on enemy aircraft even in the night skies and then started to destroy them rapidly, too many to be flukes. The British then started a propaganda campaign at the same time, saying our pilots were eating a lot of carrots and it helped them to see in the dark. Carrots were chosen as they were plentiful in Britain so it was a logical food to use. The myth still persists today!

"Cheesed Off"

Meaning: Bored, disgruntled or disgusted.

Origin: The earlier expression 'browned off', which meant the same, was RAF slang originally used of metalwork that had become rusty; it was later applied figuratively to human degeneration.

'Cheesed' is an elaboration of this, in reference to the browning of cheese when cooked, or a quite different allusion to the sourness associated with cheese going bad. The first printed use of the phrase was in 1941 from a piece in the literary digest Penguin: 'I'm browned off, I'm cheesed' but it was clearly an expression in common use by this time as we see a year later in the novel 'The Nine Lives of Bill Nelson' (1942):

"Two people, both cheesed off, are better than one."

"Fly by the Seat of One's Pants"

Meaning: Using only instinct, visual observation and practical judgment.

Origin: 'Fly by the seat of your pants' is parlance from the early days of aviation. Aircraft initially had few navigation aids and flying was accomplished by means of the pilot's judgment. The term emerged in the 1930s and was first widely used in reports of Douglas Corrigan's flight from the USA to Ireland in 1938.

That flight was reported in many US newspapers of the day, including a piece, titled 'Corrigan Flies by the Seat of His Pants', in The Edwardsville Intelligencer, 19 July 1938.

"Shot Your Bolt"

Meaning: To have already achieved all that you have the power, ability or strength to do and to be unable to do more.

Origin: The first expression comes from archery and referred to using up all of one's bolts which were short, heavy arrows fired with a crossbow. It was a proverb by the 1200s.

The colloquial variant, dating from the 1800s, comes from gambling and refers to spending all of a wad of rolled-up banknotes, this is thought to have led to another saying 'shot your wad' which is recognised in the American slang dictionary from 1814.

"In the Nick of Time"

Meaning: Only just in time.

Origin: The phrase used to be 'In the nick' and dates back to the 1500s, when nick meant the critical moment. A nick-stick was used to keep track of time, points and transactions that took place. It was especially useful in sporting events. A nick is a is a very small and precise notch that is used as a marker on a tool similar to a metre stick, known previously as a tally stick, ancient tally sticks have been used to mark things back for millennia, early examples of bones being for this purpose have been discovered in Africa and are thought to be 40,000 years old.

Pliny the Elder (AD 23–79) can be found mentioning the best wood for tallies and these measuring devices have been referenced multiple times since.

"A Turn-Up for the Books"

Meaning: A surprising or an unexpected event, often a piece of good fortune.

Origin: The origin of this idiom is in horse racing, where the book was the record of bets laid on a race kept by a bookmaker. When a horse performed in a way that nobody expected it was something that benefited the book and so the bookmaker. An up-turn for the bookmaker's luck and a 'turn up for the books'

The earliest example found of the expression in print is from a report in the Leeds Intelligencer newspaper, of the success of a horse called Blackdown at the Doncaster races in August 1863:

"A rare turn-up for the book-makers, the majority of whom had never written Blackdown's name in their books."

"Put the Cat Amongst the Pigeons"

Meaning: To say or do something that causes trouble.

Origin: Although an English idiom, the name of a Hercule Poirot film and an Agatha Christie novel which made the idiom far more popular when it was written in 1939 this idiom is believed to have derived in colonial India (1858–1918).

In this period in India, it was a popular pass time to put a wild cat in a pen with pigeons. Bets would be made on how many birds the cat would bring down.

"Xmas"

Meaning: Christmas festival period.

Origin: Xmas (also X-mas) is a common abbreviation of the word Christmas. The 'X' comes from the Greek letter Chi, which is the first letter of the Greek word *Christós* (Greek: *Χριστός*), which became Christ in English. The suffix 'mas' is from the Latin-derived Old English word for Mass. The abbreviation predates (by centuries) its use in gaudy advertisements. It was first used in English in the mid-1500s.

"Boxing Day"

Meaning: The day after Christmas day.

Origin: Boxing Day got its name when Queen Victoria was on the throne in the 1800s and has nothing to do with the sport of boxing.

The name comes from a time when the rich used to box up gifts to give to the poor. Boxing Day was traditionally a day off for servants, and the day when they received a special Christmas box from their masters. The servants would also go home on Boxing Day to give Christmas boxes to their families. The Oxford English Dictionary gives the earliest attestations from Britain in the 1830s.

"Freeze the Balls off a Brass Monkey"

Meaning: cold weather.

Origin: The most common theory, although there are others is that the term is of nautical origin. Cannonballs used to be stored in piles aboard warships in the sixteenth to eighteenth centuries, on a brass frame or tray called a 'monkey'. In very cold weather, the brass would contract, spilling the cannonballs. Hence, very cold weather is 'cold enough to freeze the balls off a brass monkey'.

The earliest example in print is in Charles Augustus Abbey's diary, 'Before the Mast in the Clippers' (1857):

"Whew, ain't it a blowing 'Jehosaphat Bumstead and cold', it would freeze the tail off of a brass monkey."

The first time there is a reference to cannons is in an inventory published in 1650 – The articles of the rendition of Edenburgh-Castle to the Lord Generall Cromwel:

"Short Brasse Munkeys alias Dogs."

At this time, the cannons themselves were known as brass monkeys. While we cannot be certain of the exact origin, most experts agree it is of nautical origin and that it refers to cold weather at sea effecting the cannons.

"Doubting Thomas"

Meaning: A person who is sceptical and refuses to believe something without proof.

Origin: The term 'a doubting Thomas' is a direct reference to the biblical story of the apostle Thomas, who refused to believe that the resurrected Jesus had been seen by the other apostles until he could actually see and feel the wounds Jesus received during his crucifixion.

The term is thought to have come from artist impressions on the subject and was formerly referred to as 'The Incredulity of Saint Thomas' which can be seen as early as the sixth century, when it appears in the mosaics at Basilica of Sant Apollinare Nuovo in Ravenna.

The first time we see the exact phrase itself, however, is not until the 1883 rendition of the bible:

"St Thomas, apostle who doubted Jesus' resurrection until he had proof of it."

"Tomfoolery"

Meaning: Foolish or silly behaviour.

Origin: Although not definitive, the 'Tom' in 'tomfoolery' is thought to be Thomas Skelton who was famous for being the last jester of Muncaster Castle in the middle of the seventeenth century. The castle is near the village of Ravenglass, Cumbria, in the north-west of England. We know this because he is the named subject of a famous full-length portrait that hangs in the castle.

The term itself gained wider popularity due to a musical revue called Tomfoolery based on lyrics and music that American mathematician, songwriter and satirist Tom Lehrer first performed in the 1950s and 1960s.

"Curiosity Killed the Cat"

Meaning: Being inquisitive about other people's affairs may get you into trouble.

Origin: The saying or phrase in its current guise was first attested in the USA in 1909. It is thought that the phrase 'curiosity killed the cat' is actually a spin-off of an old sixteenth-century saying, 'care kills a cat'.

This statement meant that cats seemed to be very cautious, careful and worrisome creatures, and too much anxiety can be bad for one's health. Over the years, the word 'care' was substituted for the word 'curiosity' in the phrase, intending to explain that this was a trait that got both people and cats into trouble sometimes!

"Hangover"

Meaning: Feeling ill after having drunk too much alcohol.

Origin: According to an article in Historic UK, the term hangover would come from the practice of homeless people in London spending the night in a room sleeping while literally hanging over a rope. Some establishments allowed people to lean on the rope while sitting on a bench, while other only allowed people to stand and lean on the taught rope. The usual cost of these lodgings was two pence and gave us the Victorian era term of 'two-penny hangover'.

The academically accepted explanation is the mere extension of the sense of 'a survival, a thing left over from before' at least as early as 1902.

"Auld Lang Syne"

Meaning: Translated literally it means 'old long since', but the meaning is more like 'old times' or 'the olden days' in old Scottish language.

Origin: In 1788, Robert Burns (Scottish poet and lyricist) sent the poem 'Auld Lang Syne' to the Scots Musical Museum, indicating that it was an ancient song but that he'd been the first to record it on paper. The phrase *'auld lang syne'* roughly translates as 'for old times' sake', and the song is all about preserving old friendships and looking back over the events of the year. It is sung all over the world, evoking a sense of belonging and fellowship, tinged with nostalgia.

It has long been a much-loved Scottish tradition to sing the song just before midnight. Everyone stands in a circle holding hands, then at the beginning of the final verse ('And there's a hand my trusty friend') they cross their arms across their bodies so that their left hand is holding the hand of the person on their right, and their right hand holds that of the person on their left. When the song ends, everyone rushes to the middle, still holding hands, and probably giggling.

The phrase itself, however, *'Auld Lang Syne'* was used in similar poems by Robert Ayton (1570–1638), Allan Ramsay (1686–1757), and James Watson (1711), as well as older folk songs predating Burns.

"Pear Shaped"

Meaning: A situation that has gone awry, perhaps horribly so.

Origin: One of the manoeuvres trainee pilots in the Royal Air Force had to master, in preparation for fighting in World War II, was the 'loop de loop'. It was a difficult aerial trick and most inexperienced pilots would not keep a perfect circle all the way around but would level off at the bottom of the loop.

The loop de loop would have a distorted outline, much to the pilot's frustration who would have to land and bare the insults from his friends that his attempt went all pear-shaped not circular as a good loop should look.

The phrase really took off in popularity though in the 1940s – in the 1940 film, My Little Chickadee starring WC Fields and Mae West, the line:

"I have some very definite pear-shaped ideas" appears – which gives a clue as to how the phrase became more widespread.

"Don't Bite off More Than You Can Chew"

Meaning: Don't take on a commitment one cannot fulfil.

Origin: This saying dates back to the 1870s in America but is probably older. It was common practice to chew tobacco at this time and people would offer others a bite of their tobacco block, if someone greedily took a bigger bite than they would chew it would be noticed. People would forewarn others not to bite off more than you can chew.

The first I can find in print of this phrase is in John Hanson Beadle's 'Western Wilds' (1877):

"I was down as Manchester the day the hauled down the stars an' stripes, an' sez I, 'Men, you've bit off more'n you can chaw;' an' they laughed at me."

"Bring Home the Bacon" and "Chew the Fat"

Meaning: Supply material support and to chat in a leisurely and prolonged way.

Origin: These sayings are very old and are said to date back as far as the twelfth century.

The theory is that towards the end of the winter, when their own food stocks were quite low, a family could obtain a piece of salted pork, which would tide them over and was seen as a luxury.

When guests would visit, Families would hang up this 'bacon', which at the time meant any meat, to display their 'wealth'. They would often cut off a chunk of this highly cured meat to share with guests and then they would sit around and 'chew the fat'.

Why bacon? It is thought this may come from a story in 1104 where a couple impressed the Prior of Little Dumlow so much with their marital devotion that he awarded them a side of bacon, a great treat at the time. This tradition continued every four years with couples showing their devotion in the town winning bacon and it is authenticated by Geoffrey Chaucer in 'The Wife of Bath's Tale' 1395: "But never for us the flitch of bacon though, that some may win in Essex at Dunmow." This tradition still takes place today.

The exact term 'Bring home the bacon' may have its traditions hundreds of years ago but is not recognised in its current wording until the turn of the twentieth century. The first seen in print is in the New York newspaper 'The Post-Standard' relating to a boxing match, 1906: "Joe, the eyes of the world are on you. Everybody says you ought to win. Peter Jackson will tell me the news and you bring home the bacon."

Again, the origins of 'chew the fat' are thought to be of the same era but is not recognised in its current wording until The Oxford English Dictionary, 1885 in a book by J Brunlees Patterson called 'Life in the Ranks of the British Army in India'.

"Upper Crust"

Meaning: Belonging to or characteristic of the upper class.

Origin: The saying 'Upper crust' entered English in the fifteenth century when Bread was an important commodity and was divvied up according to status. Indentured servants, slaves and the like got the often burnt bottom of the loaf, the family got the middle and guests, if any, got the top and best tasting 'upper crust'.

The first time the bread terminology can be found in print is in John Russell's 'The Boke of Nurture, Folowyng Englondis Gise', circa 1460:

"Kutt ye vpper crust for youre souerayne," which translates to *'Cut the upper crust of the loaf for your sovereign'*.

"Cool as a Cucumber"

Meaning: Calm and composed.

Origin: This idiom is based on the fact that in hot weather the inside of cucumbers remains cooler than the air. Despite sounding like a modern-day phrase, 'Cool as a cucumber' actually first appeared in John Gay's Poems, 'New Song on New Similies', in 1732:

"I, cool as a cucumber could see the rest of womankind."

"Hair of the Dog That Bit You"

Meaning: A colloquial expression in the English language predominantly used to refer to alcohol that is consumed with the aim of lessening the effects of a hangover.

Origin: This term for a hangover cure is another medieval saying, originating from the belief that once bitten by a rabid dog, the victim would be cured by applying the same dog's hair to the wound.

The first use of it being applied to drinking was in John Heywood's 1546 tome 'A Dialogue Conteinyng the Nomber in Effect of all the Prouerbes in the Englishe Tongue':

"I pray thee let me and my fellow have, a hair of the dog that bit us last night, and bitten were we both to the brain aright, we saw each other drunk in the good ale glass."

Strangely enough, whilst the hair of the dog is now medically dismissed as a treatment for rabies there is some truth in additional alcohol being a cure for a hangover in that part of the ill feeling is due to withdrawal symptoms.

"Off the Record"

Meaning: Not made as an official or attributable statement.

Origin: This American phrase was first attributed to President Franklin Roosevelt in 1932, who was recorded in 'The Daily Times' newspaper saying,

"He was going to talk 'off the record', that it was mighty nice to be able to talk 'off the record' for a change and that he hoped to be able to talk 'off the record' often in the future."

"Frog in the Throat"

Meaning: To be unable to speak normally because one's throat is dry and hoarse. Origin: The phrase itself is thought to be quite logical in that someone with a sore throat sounds 'croaky', like a frog. The earliest use of this name for a sore throat in print is by American clergyman Harvey Newcomb,1847:

"Now let me beg of you to learn to say NO. If you find a 'frog in your throat,' which obstructs your utterance, go by yourself, and practise saying no, no, no."

We can also see by 1894 the term is widespread enough to be in 'The Stevens Point Journal' where we can actually see the Taylor Brothers advertising a 'frog in the throat' lozenge as a 'cure' for hoarseness at 10cents a box.

"Saved by the Bell"

Meaning: Saved at the last moment.

Origin: Experts believe this saying comes from an old custom of burying coffins with a bell attached as fear of being buried alive was widespread. The thought was if someone awoke, they could use the bell to alert people they were alive. George Washington, first US president, displayed this fear and is quoted as saying:

"Have me decently buried, but do not let my body be put into a vault in less than two days after I am dead."

Early examples of these 'safety coffins' with bells attached can be seen in designs by Franz Vester in 1868 although it is thought they were built earlier.

"Hats off to You"

Meaning: The removal of one's hat is typically a gesture of respect.

Origin: Throughout history, hats identified social standing and removing a hat was a gesture of respect. In the 'old days', men took off their hats in Christian churches, when they entered someone's home, when greeting a boss, and always in the presence of a lady. A woodcut of King Charles I of England dining at Whitehall provides a clue to the answer. The only person wearing a hat at the table is the king himself. Removing your hat was a sign of respect, specifically a gesture that denoted you were deferring to someone of higher status and there was no one of higher status than the king and his crown.

Although taking your hat off has clearly been a mark of respect for centuries, the phrase itself cannot be found in print until the mid-1800s.

"Swings and Roundabouts"

Meaning: A situation in which different actions or options result in no eventual gain or loss.

Origin: P.G. Wodehouse's book *Love among the Chickens*, which was published in 1906 states:

"A man must go through the fire before he writes his masterpiece. We learn in suffering what we teach in song. What we lose on the swings, we make up on the roundabouts."

It is a reference to financial loss and gain in that what you lose on one you gain on the other.

Writer Patrick Reginald Chalmers (1872–1942) famous for biographies of several literary figures, including author of Peter Pan J. M. Barrie, and The Wind in the Willows author, Kenneth Grahame, popularised the saying six years later in a poem entitled 'Roundabouts and Swings', which was first published in Chalmers' volume Green Days and Blue Days in 1912. The poem had the line below:

"Was joggin' in the dust along 'is roundabouts and swings. An' losses on the roundabouts means profits on the swings!"

"Not My Cup of Tea"

Meaning: Not what one likes or is interested in.

Origin: In keeping with the high regard for tea, most of the early references to 'a cup of tea' as a description of an acquaintance are positive ones, that is, 'nice', 'good', 'strong' etc. The expression is more often used in the 'not my cup of tea' from these days.

This negative usage began in WWII. An early example of it is found in Hal Boyle's 'Leaves from a War Correspondent's Notebook' column, which described English life and manners for an American audience. The column provided the American counterpart to Alister Cooke's 'Letter from America' and was syndicated in various US papers. In 1944, he wrote:

"You don't say someone gives you a pain in the neck. You just remark 'He's not my cup of tea'."

The change from the earlier positive 'my cup of tea' phrase, to the dismissive 'not my cup of tea' doesn't reflect the national taste for the drink itself. Tea remains our cup of tea here in the UK. According to the United Kingdom Tea Council, 60 million of us down 160 million cups of the stuff each day.

"Until the Cows Come Home"

Meaning: A very long time.

Origin: The origin of the phrase 'til the cows come home' comes from the practice of cows returning to their shelters at some indefinite point, usually at a slow, languid pace. Cattle let out to pasture may only be expected to return for milking the next morning. Thus, for example, a party that goes on 'until the cows come home' is a very long one.

The first example found in print is by John Eliot in Ortho-epia Gallica, 1593, which was a French teaching textbook:

"I am tied by the foote till the Cow come home."

"Ditto"

Meaning: Indicates that something already said is applicable a second time.

Origin: It comes from the Italian word ditto, a dialect variation on detto, meaning 'said', (or 'What you said') the past participle of dice, 'to say'. It was used in Italian as in il ditto libro, 'the aforesaid book'. In English, it came to be used in the seventeenth century to avoid having to repeat words and phrases in accounting and commercial language.

"Bat Sh*t Crazy"

Meaning: A person that is completely insane.

Origin: This saying comes from a popular phrase from around the turn of the twentieth century, to 'have bats in the belfry'. Old-fashioned churches had a structure at the top called a belfry, which housed the church bells. Bats are highly sensitive to sounds and would not inhabit any belfry of an active church where the bell was being rung often.

When a church became abandoned and many years would pass without the bell being rung, bats would eventually inhabit the belfry. So, when somebody said that an individual had 'bats in the belfry' it meant that there was 'nothing going on upstairs'. From there, we get terms like 'batty' and 'gone bats'.

During the Vietnam War, military slang turned 'bats' and 'batty' to 'batsh*t'. The earliest surviving usage is from Lt William Calley (of the My Lai massacre) who was quoted in 1971 saying,

*"Most of America's males were in Korea or World War II or I. They killed, and they aren't all going batsh*t."*

The earliest usage of the full term 'batsh*t crazy' that can be found is a P.S. Mueller cartoon from 1983.

"Spitting Image"

Meaning: Someone or something that looks very much like someone or something else.

Origin: The initial reason given for why we should have used 'spit' in this manner is that it was said of a child that he or she looked enough like a parent to have been the 'spit out of their mouth'. Spit has been so used since at least the late sixteenth century. The earliest recorded version found is in William Charke's 'An Answeare for the Time', 1583:

"As like the papists, as if they had beene spit out of their mouthes." The concept and phrase were in clear circulation however by 1689, when George Farquhar used it in his play Love and a Bottle:

"Poor child! He's as like his own dada as if he were spit out of his mouth."

"Throwing Your Hat into the Ring"

Meaning: Express willingness to take up a challenge.

Origin: The ring in question here is a boxing ring. These, of course used to be circular spaces in a crowd of onlookers, rather than the square, roped 'rings' we see today. Anybody who fancied their chances in a bout would throw in their hat in the ring. This was a more reliable way of putting oneself forward than just shouting over the noise of the crowd. The expression dates from at least the early nineteenth century.

The earliest example seen in print is from an 1805 issue of 'The Sporting Magazine': "Belcher appeared confident of success and threw his hat into the ring, as an act of defiance to his antagonist."

"The Real Mccoy"

Meaning: The real thing; the genuine article.

Origin: There are numerous theories for this particular idiom. One is that it is derived from a Scottish whisky company called McKay and we see the first example of this in the Scottish poem 'Deil's Hallowe'en' (1856):

"A drop of the real McKay."

The other main and most popular theory which is correct in name is that 'The real McCoy' was the inventor Elijah McCoy, born in Canada in 1844. He had many different inventions including an ironing board and a lawn sprinkler but most famously made a machine for lubricating engines. The first printed example of 'The real McCoy' can be seen in print in Canada so it is a logical leap of faith that as Elijah was Canadian, the saying is based on him.

Canadian James S. Bond's wrote in his novel 'The Rise and Fall of the Union Club' (1881):

"By jingo, yes, so it will be. It's the 'real McCoy', as Jim Hicks says."

"A Whale of a Time"

Meaning: A very enjoyable experience.

Origin: This idiom alludes to the largest mammal to describe something very large and impressive. In the early 1900s 'a whale of' something was simply an intensifier.

'A whale of a time' might be the most common use of this structure, but it's possible to encounter this phrase in other contexts too. A whale of a man, if he was big or a whale of a brain, if they were smart are two other examples. 'A Dictionary of American Student Slang' by Willard C. Gore records 'whale' in 1895 as 'a person who is a prodigy either physically or intellectually', or 'something exceptionally large'.

"That Old Chestnut"

Meaning: A story that has been told repeatedly before, a 'venerable' joke.

Origin: The phrase 'old chestnut' has only an indirect association with chestnut trees or with their fruit. In 1816, a melodrama called Broken Sword, by the playwright and theatrical manager William Dimond, was performed at the Royal Covent Garden Theatre, London. The play contained this exchange:

Zavior: "I entered the wood at Collares, when suddenly from the thick boughs of a cork tree."
Pablo: (Jumping up.) "A chestnut, Captain, a chestnut... Captain, this is the twenty-seventh time I have heard you relate this story, and you invariably said, a chestnut, till now."

The reference being Pablo repeating the same story again and again. Despite a drubbing from the critics, the play was a success and later transferred to theatres in the USA.

"The Acid Test"

Meaning: A conclusive test of the success or value of something.

Origin: This term came from the California Gold Rush in the nineteenth century, when prospectors and dealers used nitric acid to distinguish gold from base metal, relying on the acids ability to dissolve metals other than gold more readily. The test itself was developed in the late eighteenth century but the phrase became popular in the Gold rush itself, 1848–55.

The first printed version of the phrase where the figurative meaning is used rather than an actual physical test involving acid can be seen in the Wisconsin paper 'The Columbia Reporter', 1845: "Twenty-four years of service demonstrates his ability to stand the acid test."

"Every Tom, Dick and Harry"

Meaning: Anyone and everyone.

Origin: The origin of the idiom is unknown and dating the first use is problematic too, depending on which source you believe. Oxford English Dictionary has the first use in 1657 by the English religious thinker John Owen. HarperCollins has it as 1734. Shakespeare used the variation 'Tom, Dick and Francis' in Act 1 of Henry IV, 1583–97. What we can say for sure is that the saying is at least 400 years old based on the Shakespeare play but it probably dates back much earlier than this. The strongest theory is that Thomas, Richard and Henry were very common names in medieval times, with their pet names Tom, Dick, Harry. When you wanted to say that a plan, a course of action or a thing that may appeal to large numbers of the populace, you say every Tom, Dick and Harry would like that. The implication was that these were not the richest or socially most important people, but common people whom you would normally call by pet name, not formal ones.

"Keeping Up with the Joneses"

Meaning: Try to emulate or not be outdone by one's neighbours.

Origin: This American term emerged in 1913, when Arthur (Pop) Momand started a *Keep up with the Joneses* comic strip in the New York Globe. The comic strip was about family life in a street in America. The strip was so popular, that in 1915 a cartoon film of the same name was released.

"Jack S**t"

Meaning: Nothing at all.

Origin: There are a number of theories with where this phrase originates but the popular theory is that in British English, Jack has been around since the thirteenth century as a term to designate the average peasant or the average man. During the British naval supremacy period, Jack was also used to designate the average seaman ('Jack Tar'), and is still used today. The word passed into American English in examples such as 'lumberjack s**t' is a symbol of something of little value, the use of jack here is an intensifier referring to an average fellow of supposedly low level of sophistication or knowledge, or someone that meant nothing to the wealthy.

It is not until the 1960s that we see 'Jack s**t' for the first time being used as slang for nothing. Although there is no definitive origin this is the most logical theory according to experts.

"Got Away with Blue Murder" and "Screaming Blue Murder"

Meaning: 'Getting away with blue murder' implies a person has got away with something so bad that they were expected to get caught for. 'Screaming blue murder' is to scream, yell or complain in a very loud or angry way.

Origin: The murder of royalty, or 'blue-bloods', was historically exceptionally heinous and difficult to get away with. So, if someone 'got away with blue murder', they were quite lucky or very devious. The word 'blue' in English also has a history of being used to stress or strengthen an expression, as in 'blue blazes' or 'bolt from the blue' hence blue murder meaning exceptional murder or screaming blue murder meaning screaming exceptionally loud.

In 1834, the Anglo-Irish children's writer Maria Edgeworth published a novel entitled Helen which is where we see 'Blue bloods' referring to royalty is first in print.

"Basket Case"

Meaning: A person or thing regarded as useless or unable to cope.

Origin: This term was used by the US military after WWI, referring to soldiers who had lost arms and legs and had to be carried by others. The Online Etymology Dictionary confirms that 'basket case', which it dates to the US in 1919, originally referred to quadriplegics who had suffered catastrophic wounds in the first world war, adding grimly that this was probably literal as in stuck in a basket.

"A Baker's Dozen"

Meaning: A group or set of thirteen items or units.

Origin: This phrase is widely believed to originate from medieval times, when English bakers gave an extra loaf when selling a dozen in order to avoid being penalised for selling a short weight. Bakers could be fined, pilloried or flogged for selling 'underweight' bread.

The law that caused bakers to be so wary was the 'Assize of Bread and Ale'. In 1266, Henry III revived an ancient statute that regulated the price of bread according to the price of wheat.

The action of extra bread being given to avoid being penalised is older than the phrase however and the first printed version can be seen in John Cooke's 'Tu Quoque', 1599:

"Mine's a baker's dozen, Master Bubble, tell your money."

"A Penny for Your Thoughts"

Meaning: Used to ask someone what they are thinking about.

Origin: The first printed version of this phrase can be found in 1522 in Sir Thomas Moore's book 'Four Last Things'. It was a book of meditations on death, God's judgement, pain and how to combat 'spiritual diseases':

"As it often happeth that the very face sheweth the mind walking a pilgrimage, in such wise that, not without some note and reproach of such vagrant mind, other folk suddenly say to them, 'A penny for your thought'."

The book alludes to a wise man falling silent and he needs to be paid in order to garner his wisdom, similar to what the meaning is to this day. The saying didn't seem to gain popularity until a while after when famous writer John Heywood wrote in his book titled 'Proverbs and Epigrams of John Heywood' (1547):

"Freend, a peny for your thought."

"Making a Right Pig's Ear of It"

Meaning: Completely botch something up or make a complete mess of it.

Origin: 'Make a pig's ear' is a mid-twentieth-century phrase. This is first found in print in its current guise in a 1950 edition of the Reader's Digest:

"If you make a pig's ear of the first one, you can try the other one." The expression derives from the old proverb 'you can't make a silk purse out of a sow's ear', which dates from the sixteenth century. The English clergyman Stephen Gosson published the romantic story Ephemerides in 1579 and in it referred to people who were engaged in a hopeless task:

"Seekinge too make a silke purse of a Sowes eare."

"Get the Sack"

Meaning: To be dismissed suddenly from a job.

Origin: This slang term for getting fired originates in France, and alludes to tradesmen, who would take their own bag or 'sac', in French, of tools with them when dismissed from employment. It has been known in France since the seventeenth century, as '*On luy a donné son sac*'. The first recorded English version is in Charles Westmacott's The English Spy, 1825:

"You munna split on me, or I shall get the zack for telling on ye."

"Purple Patch"

Meaning: A run of success or good luck.

Origin: From the late sixteenth century, 'purple' has been used to mean 'striking' or 'ornate', this can quite often be seen in Royal garments. 'Purple patches', which are also sometimes called 'purple passages' or 'purple prose', were originally a figurative reference to florid literary passages, added to a text for dramatic effect. In 1598, Queen Elizabeth translated Horace's Latin text '*De Arte Poetica*' and this was published in 1899 as part of Queen Elizabeth's Englishings:

"Oft to beginnings graue and shewes of great is sowed A purple pace, one or more for vewe."

The term 'Purple patch' is not seen again until the 1704 book 'The True Tom Double':

"The Purple Patches he claps upon his Course Style make it seem much Courser than it is."

It wasn't until the twentieth century that 'purple patches' were used in relation to anything other than writing. The term then came to mean 'a period of good fortune or creativity'. The first example I can find in print of the figurative meaning is in 'The Westminster Budget', 1900:

"True, it is hardly to be counted a purple patch of history."

"I Smell a Rat"

Meaning: One is suspicious of something or someone.

Origin: This phrase is said to come from the sixteenth century in the days when rats were common pests and carriers of disease in England. Dogs were prized for their ability to smell out and destroy them. A dog which began to sniff around might well have smelt a rat, and this idea was transferred to a person who was suspicious of something. The first known use of this phrase is in 'The Image of Ipocrysy', an anonymous poem written around 1540:

"Must sey that white is blacke, or elles they sey we smacke, and smell we wote not what, but then beware the catt, for yf they smell a ratt."

"The Proof Is in the Pudding"

Meaning: Success or effectiveness of something can only be determined by putting it to the test.

Origin: 'The proof is in the pudding' is a new twist on a very old proverb. The original version is 'the proof of the pudding is in the eating'. The saying 'the proof of the pudding is in the eating' is first recorded in English in William Camden's 'Remaines of a Greater Worke Concerning Britaine' (1605):

"All the proof of a pudding is in the eating."

Phrases for the notion that to taste something is to test it go back to the fourteenth century in the UK according to the Oxford English Dictionary although there is nothing solid with this precise phrase. In this era, the 'puddings' were not the delicious confectionary we see. Puddings were essentially sausages, usually mixtures of minced meat, cereal and spices.

"Straight from the Horse's Mouth"

Meaning: Heard from the person who has direct personal knowledge of something or the person themselves.

Origin: In horse racing circles, tips on which horse is a likely winner circulate amongst punters. The most trusted authorities are considered to be those in closest touch with the recent form of the horse, that is, stable lads, trainers etc. The notional 'from the horse's mouth' is supposed to indicate the best tip possible, a tip from the horse itself. The earliest instance found is from 'Bell's Life in London and Sporting Chronicle' of Sunday 22 September 1861.

"Rank Outsider. A raker to win, straight from the horse's mouth and two steamers for places."

"Lazy Bones" and "Bone Idle"

Meaning: A lazy person.

Origin: The origin of both are very old and due to the concept of just the depth of idleness or laziness of someone, that there is nothing deeper in a limb than a bone. 'Lazy bones' and the newer saying 'bone idle' mean the same thing and the earliest written examples of these are: Lazy bones, 1593, in G. Harvey Pierce's 'Supererogation': *"Was legierdemane a sloweworme, or Viuacitie a lasie-bones."*

Bone idle, 1836, in T. Carlyle's 'New Lett': *"For the last three weeks, I have been going what you call bone-idle."*

"Cloud Cuckoo Land"

Meaning: A state of absurdly, over-optimistic fantasy.

Origin: This ancient saying dates from 414 BC, in a play called 'The Birds', written by the Greek comic playwright Aristophanes. The play was first translated into English by the poet and translator Henry F. Cary, in 1824, which is the date 'cloud-cuckoo-land' entered the language. The translation directly from the ancient play reads as below: *Pisthetairos: All right then, what name shall we provide?*

Chorus leader: Some name from around here , to do with clouds, with high places full of air, something really extra grand.
Pisthetairos: Well, then, how do you like this: Cloudcuckooland?

"Gung Ho"

Meaning: Unthinkingly enthusiastic and eager.

Origin: Gung-ho describes enthusiasm – often to the point of naïveté. But it didn't always. The original Chinese is 工業合作社, which means "industrial cooperative' – 工業, (gōng yè) meaning 'industry', and 合作社, (hé zuò shè) meaning 'cooperative'. We're talking about organisations democratically run by workers here, producing industrial goods like blankets and military uniforms. 工業合作社 was abbreviated, as many long Chinese proper nouns are, to the first character of each part, 工合. Today, we would Romanise it to gōng hé, but in the 1930s, the same sounds turned into kung ho, or gung-ho and was adopted as a slogan by US Marines and was used in its current context.

"Apple of My Eye"

Meaning: Special favourite, beloved person or thing.

Origin: The apple of one's eye originally referred to the central aperture of the eye. Figuratively it is something, or more usually someone, cherished above others. 'The apple of my eye' is an exceedingly old expression which first appears, in Old English, in a work attributed to King Alfred the Great of Wessex, AD 885, titled 'Gregory's Pastoral Care':

"Poor Richard was to me as an eldest son, the apple of my eye." Much later, Shakespeare used the phrase in 'A Midsummer Night's Dream', 1600:

"Flower of this purple dye, Hit with Cupid's archery, Sink in apple of his eye."

It also appears several times in the Bible, for example, in Deuteronomy 32:10 (King James Version, 1611)

"He found him in a desert land, and in the waste howling wilderness; he led him about, he instructed him, he kept him as the apple of his eye."

"Scot Free"

Meaning: Without suffering any punishment or injury.

Origin: 'Skat' is a Scandinavian word for tax or payment and the word migrated to Britain and mutated into 'scot' as the name of a redistributive taxation, levied as early the tenth century as a form of municipal poor relief. No one likes paying tax and people have been getting off scot-free since at least the eleventh century. The first reference in print to 'scot free' is in a forged copy of the Writ of Edward the Confessor. There is no precise date for the forged version of the writ but Edward died in 1066 and the copy was made sometime in the thirteenth century.

"A Feather in One's Cap"

Meaning: An achievement to be proud of.

Origin: It is believed that the Native American warriors/braves would add a feather to the head dress of the warriors who have been brave. Hungarians hundreds of years ago would also add a feather in their caps each time when they have killed an enemy in war. The number of feather's suggested bravery and nationalism. In literature, the phrase has been first known to be used since 1599, by Richard Hansard in his book Description of Hungary. In the United Kingdom, this phrase became popular in the eighteenth century when the Duchess of Portland used it in her letter to Miss Collingwood.

"Teaching Granny to Suck Eggs"

Meaning: Giving advice to another person on a subject with which the other person is already familiar.

Origin: The meaning of the idiom derives from the fact that before the creation of modern dentistry many elderly people had very bad teeth, or no teeth. The simplest way for them to eat protein was to poke a pinhole in the shell of a raw egg and suck out the contents; therefore, a grandmother was usually already a practiced expert on sucking eggs and didn't need anyone to show her how to do it. Though the practice may be much older, the earliest scripted version found is from 'The History of Tom Jones, a Foundling' by Henry Fielding (1749):

"I remember my old schoolmaster, who was a prodigious great scholar, used often to say, Polly matete cry town is my daskalon. The English of which, he told us, was, that a child may sometimes teach his grandmother to suck eggs."

"Eat Your Heart Out"

Meaning: Suffer from excessive longing for someone or something unattainable.

Origin: This saying was a favourite Jewish expression in show business circles during the twentieth century but was certainly used much earlier. Diogenes Laertius credited Pythagoras with saying 'Do not eat your heart', meaning don't waste your life worrying about something, this reference is circa 500 BC.

"In a Pickle"

Meaning: A difficult position or problem to which no easy answer can be found.
Origin: The earliest pickles were spicy sauces made to accompany meat dishes.
Later, in the sixteenth century, the name pickle was also given to a mixture of
spiced, salted vinegar that was used as a preservative. The word comes from the
Dutch or Low German pekel, with the meaning of something piquant. The 'in
trouble' meaning of 'in a pickle' was an allusion to being as confused or mixed
up as the stewed vegetables that made up pickles. There were stories in the
seventeenth century related to hapless people who found themselves on the
menu. A famous early example in print was by none other than Shakespeare who
was one of the first to use 'in a pickle', in 'The Tempest' (1610):

*ALONSO: And Trinculo is reeling ripe: where should they find this grand liquor
that hath gilded 'em? How camest thou in this pickle?*
*TRINCULO: I have been in such a pickle since I saw you last that, I fear me, will
never out of my bones: I shall not fear fly-blowing.*

"Suits Me to a T"

Meaning: Perfectly or exactly right.
Origin: 'To a T' or 'To a Tee', meaning 'exactly', 'precisely' or 'perfectly' is an
old expression, dating all the way back to the late seventeenth century, here is an
early written example:
*"All the under Villages and Towns-men come to him for Redress, which he does
to a T."* (1693) The 'T' in 'to a T' was originally short for a word beginning with
'T' – 'Tittle', meaning 'a very small part of something' or 'a very small amount'.
'To a tittle', meaning exactly the same thing as 'to a T', was in common use
almost a century before 'to a T' appeared.

"Abracadabra"

Meaning: A word said by conjurers when performing a magic trick.

Origin: No one is certain as to the origin of the strange word 'abracadabra'. The word itself, however, is of Aramaic origin. *'Avra kadavra'*, meaning 'it will be created in my words'. It is known to have been in use in fourth-century Latin in the *Avra kadavra* wording. The first reference in print to the use of the word in English dating back to 1582 is found in Eva Rimmington Taylor's 'The Troublesome Voyage of Capt. Edward Fenton':

"Banester sayth yt he healed 200 in one yer of an ague by hanging abracadabra about their necks."

What we can say is that the word is ancient, goes back to at least the fourth century in its original form and meant to create, which suits the word being 'Magic'.

"Heard It Through the Grapevine"

Meaning: Something found out unofficially rather than through an official announcement.

Origin: The term originated in the USA and comes from the telegraph system invented in the nineteenth century by Samuel Morse. People thought the wires and poles looked like the strings attached to grapevines and then the term 'Grapevine telegraph' was first coined in 1852 in a US dictionary. During the American Civil War, 1861–65, rumours were often spread via the telegraph lines. When people were asked whether a particular story was true, they would often reply 'I heard it through the grapevine'.

The saying really came into its own in popularity however following the hit song 'heard it through the grapevine' by Gladys Knight and the pips in 1967 and then Marvin Gaye in 1968.

"Smarty Pants"

Meaning: A derogatory term used for someone who thinks they are clever, a know-it-all.

Origin: The origin of the term 'Smarty Pants' derives from 'smarty', which first surfaced in a California magazine in 1861: 'Juvenile smarties are interesting even to a vagabond' was the name of the story. The term 'smarty' was also used in Tom Sawyer by Mark Twain in 1876. The first use of 'smarty pants' seems to be in 1941 by B. Schulenberg in 'What makes Sammy Run?':

"One of those Vassar smartypants." The pants was added as an intensifier to many words in the mid-twentieth century, another example being 'Fancy pants'.

"The Best Thing Since Sliced Bread"

Meaning: Used to emphasise one's enthusiasm about a new idea, person or thing.

Origin: Otto Frederick Rohwedder of Davenport, Iowa, United States, invented the first single loaf bread-slicing machine. A prototype he built in 1912 was destroyed in a fire and it was not until 1928 that Rohwedder had a fully working machine ready. The first commercial use of the machine was by the Chillicothe Baking Company of Chillicothe, Missouri, which sold their first slices on 7 July 1928. Their product, 'Kleen Maid Sliced Bread', proved to be a success. It was first sold in 1928, advertised as 'the greatest forward step in the baking industry since bread was wrapped'. This led to the popular idiom 'greatest thing since sliced bread'.

"The Devil Is in the Details"

Meaning: Something might seem simple at a first look but may take more time and effort to complete than expected.

Origin: The source of the proverb 'The devil is in the details' is often attributed to the German/American architect Ludwig Mies Van Der Rohe. This is almost certainly a misattribution. The expression derives from an earlier German proverb: "*Der liebe Gott steckt im detail*," which translates as 'God is in the detail'. Mies Van Der Rohe is also associated with this earlier form but there is no proof of this. It is assumed, however, that this is where the saying originated. 'The devil is in the details' only came into common use in the 1990s (Van Der Rohe died in 1969) and the earliest citation of it found in print is in Richard Mayne's explanation of the workings of the European Union – The Community of Europe, 1963: *"On the principle that 'the devil is in the details', what should have been a merely formal occasion developed into a debate about the Community's official languages and the site of its headquarters."*

"Run Out of Steam"

Meaning: Lose impetus or enthusiasm.

Origin: This phrase is in reference to steam engines which gradually slow and then stop when the fire that powers the boiler is too low to produce steam. The first figurative use came from the USA in the late nineteenth century. The earliest of these that can be found in print is from the Iowa newspaper 'The Perry Daily Chief' (1898):

"That made it impossible for me to get in one word to her hundred. I stood it for a little while in hope she would run out of steam or material, but she gathered force as she went."

"Killing Two Birds with One Stone"

Meaning: To achieve two things by doing a single action.

Origin: It is believed that the phrase originated from the story of Daedalus and Icarus from Greek Mythology. Daedalus killed two birds with one stone in order to get the feathers of the birds and make the wings. The father and son escaped from the Labyrinth on Crete by making wings and flying out. The story is thought to be from at least 500 BC. In 1656, the phrase, in its exact form, can be found in 'The Questions Concerning Liberty, Necessity and Chance' written by Thomas Hobbes:

"T. H. thinks to kill two birds with one stone, and satisfie two Arguments with one answer, whereas in truth he satisfieth neither."

"Hobson's Choice"

Meaning: A choice of taking what is available or nothing at all.

Origin: The phrase is thought to have originated with Thomas Hobson, 1544–1631, a livery stable owner in Cambridge, England. According to a plaque underneath a painting of Hobson donated to Cambridge Guildhall, Hobson had an extensive stable of some 40 horses. This gave the appearance to his customers that, upon entry, they would have their choice of mounts, when in fact there was only one. Hobson required his customers to choose the horse in the stall closest to the door. This was to prevent the best horses from always being chosen, which would have caused those horses to become overused. According to the Oxford English Dictionary, the first known written usage of this phrase is in 'The Rustick's alarm to the Rabbies', written by Samuel Fisher in 1660: "If in this case there be no other (as the Proverb is), then Hobson's choice, which is, choose whether you will have this or none."

"Above Board"

Meaning: legitimate, honest and open.

Origin: 'Above board' first appeared in print, in the early seventeenth century, and the phrase originated in the world of gambling, in particular card games. To play 'above board' was to keep your cards above the level of the playing table, as opposed to down in your lap, so as to avoid any suspicion of cheating.

The first version in print found of the saying can be seen in Beaumont & Fletcher's 'The Custom of the Country' (1616):

"Yet if you play not fair play and above board too."

"Tying the Knot"

Meaning: Getting married.

Origin: The phrase 'tie the knot' comes from an ancient wedding tradition, the handfasting ceremony. This ancient Celtic practice, which dates back to circa 1225, where the Middle English word 'enotte', or 'knot,' was used to mean 'the tie or bond of wedlock'. It meant to literally bind couples together in matrimony by tying knots of cloth around their hands. And so, two become one.

"Pie in the Sky"

Meaning: Describes or refers to something that is pleasant to contemplate but is very unlikely to be realised.

Origin: The phrase is originally from the song 'The Preacher and the Slave' (1911) by Swedish-American labour activist and songwriter Joe Hill (1879–1915), which he wrote as a parody of the Salvation Army hymn 'In the Sweet By-and-By' (published 1868). The song criticises the Salvation Army for focusing on people's salvation rather than on their material needs:

"You will eat, bye and bye. In that glorious land above the sky, work and pray, live on hay, you'll get pie in the sky when you die."

"Bone of Contention"

Meaning: A subject or issue over which there is continuing disagreement.

Origin: The phrase used to be 'a bone of dissension' and comes from the fact that two dogs would often fight over a bone, with neither animal wanting to give in to the other. The original phrase was used in the 1500s but changed in and around the 1700s. It is unclear whether the phrase has changed or whether the word 'dissension' just fell into disuse. There is also a possibility that it can be traced back to the phrase 'to find bones in something'. This phrase meant to find an objection to something. In both phrases, the word 'bone' means to oppose something. This phrase can be traced back to the Paston letters of 1459.

"Carry the Can"

Meaning: Take responsibility for a mistake or misdeed.

Origin: There are a number of theories on this one but the most popular is that 'carrying the can' is in fact a variation of the word 'cannee', which was an old Gaelic French military term meaning a type of tent or cover to keep gun powder dry. Soldiers who were in charge of the cannee were vital if the weather was inclement. So, to 'carry the can' meant to take responsibly for the army's fire power. This idiom is found in script in early twentieth century naval or military slang.

"Dog Eat Dog"

Meaning: Used to refer to a situation of fierce competition in which people are willing to harm each other in order to succeed.

Origin: This phrase contradicts an old Latin proverb which maintains that dog does not eat dog, first recorded in England in 1543. By 1732, it was put as 'Dogs are hard drove when they eat dogs' in Thomas Fuller's, 'Gnomologia'. The sense of the Fuller quotation and the Roman saying are much to the same effect, that dog eating dog is highly unnatural and therefore a sign of an extreme environment. The notion that, in human relations, 'it's a dog-eat-dog world out there', which presents (figuratively) canine cannibalism as an essential aspect of the normal state of the world is thus fundamentally at odds with the original sense of Fuller's saying. The phrase 'dog eat dog world' first shows up in print in Elias Tobenlin's 'The House of Conrad' in 1918.

"Double Dutch"

Meaning: Language that is impossible to understand; gibberish.

Origin: The word 'Dutch' is thought to be chosen because it denotes a language that few people can speak, like Greek in 'it's all Greek to me', and double is thought to be a mere intensifier of the notion of it being nonsensical. The earliest instance of double Dutch, unambiguously used in the current sense, that can be found in print is from 'The Bradford Observer' in 1839:

"The language is not the Danish, but the real original 'double Dutch', in which Mr Bellenden Ker's Nursery Rhymes were originally written."

"Flash in the Pan"

Meaning: A thing or person whose sudden but brief success is not repeated.
Origin: This is thought to have come from Flintlock muskets which used to have small pans to hold charges of gunpowder. An attempt to fire the musket in which the gunpowder flared up without a bullet being fired was a 'flash in the pan'. The term itself, however, has been known since the late seventeenth century. Elkanah Settle wrote in 'Reflections', a play from 1687:

"If Cannons were so well bred in his Metaphor as only to flash in the Pan, I dare lay an even wager that Mr Dryden durst venture to Sea."

"Jumping on the Bandwagon"

Meaning: To join an activity that has become very popular or to change your opinion to one that has become very popular so that you can share in its success.
Origin: The definition of a 'bandwagon' here, is a wagon which carries a band during the course of a parade, circus or other entertainment event. The phrase 'jump on the bandwagon' first appeared in American politics in 1848 when Dan Rice, a famous and popular circus clown of the time, used his bandwagon and its music to gain attention for his political campaign appearances. As his campaign became more successful, other politicians strove for a seat on the bandwagon, hoping to be associated with his success. Later, during the time of William Jennings Bryan's 1900 presidential campaign, bandwagons had become standard in campaigns, and the phrase 'jump on the bandwagon' was used as a derogatory term, implying that people were associating themselves with success without considering that with which they associated themselves.

"Just Deserts"

Meaning: Receive what one deserves, whether good or bad.

Origin: Deserts, in the sense of 'things deserved' has been used in English since at least the thirteenth century. A citation in which it is linked with 'just' comes from 1548 in Nicholas Udall's 'Translation of Erasmus'. The first tome or volume of the 'Paraphrase of Erasmus upon the Newe Testamente':

"It procedeth more of their enuie, of their unquietnes of minde ...then of any faute or just deserte in Erasmus." Deserts is now almost always used in reference to desolate and arid regions of land. Its use to mean 'that which is deserved' is now largely limited to this single phrase. Desserts meaning the last or sweet course of a meal is widely used and is pronounced the same way as the deserts in 'just deserts'. So, when hearing the phrase with the pronunciation like 'desserts', people think it must be spelled that way too. The spelling might be more intuitive if we thought of the phrase as 'what you justly deserve'.

"Laughing stock"

Meaning: A person subjected to general mockery or ridicule.

Origin: The origin of the phrase is linked with the medieval practice of putting people into stocks as a punishment for a variety of crimes. Despite the discomfort this caused those who were in the stocks, what was worse was the torture and ridicule they suffered at the hands of their fellow villagers. The laughing part of 'laughing stock', is a given, however, the word 'stock' first appeared in English in 862, adapted from the German word meaning tree trunk. What's more, at the time, the word stock meant something or someone treated as the object of an action, more or less habitually. Just as a person who was publicly scorned was referred to as a pointing stock, and a person who was frequently whipped was a whipping stock, those who were frequently laughed at were known as laughing stocks. The first printed version of the current meaning can be found in the 1533 book 'Another boke against Rastel' by John Frith, the following passage can be found:

"Albeit ... I be reputed a laughing stock in this world."

"A Load of Old Cobblers"

Meaning: Nonsense.

Origin: 'A load of old cobblers' and variants such as 'what a load of cobblers' or just 'cobblers' is British slang for 'what nonsense'. It is derived from the Cockney rhyming slang for 'b*lls', slang for testicles, or 'cobbler's awls' in full cockney rhyming slang style. A stitching awl or cobbler's awl is actually a tool with which holes can be punctured in a variety of materials. The use of 'cobblers' as a synonym for b*lls dates back to at least the 1930s although the term 'load of old cobblers' and similar variants only gained wide popularity from the 1960s and British sitcom Steptoe and Son (1962–74) really brought the saying to the fore.

"Mum's the Word"

Meaning: Used to say that some information is being kept secret or should be kept secret.

Origin: The word 'mum' is a slanged version of another word, 'momme' or 'mom', which was used between 1350–1400 in Middle English with very close to the same meaning, be silent, do not reveal and has nothing to do with someone's mother. The first printed version of the phrase with the original word can be found in the fourteenth-century poem by William Langland, 'The vision of William concerning Piers Plowman':

"Then geten a mom of heore mouth til moneye weore schewed." You can see the word 'mum' it in its more modern spelt version in Shakespeare's 'Henry VI, Part 2' written 1589–92:

"Seal up your lips and give no words but mum."

The first in print version of the full saying is seen in 'A Walk Around London and Westminster' by Thomas Brown, 1720:

"But Mum's the Word – for who would speak their Mind among Tarrs and Commissioners."

"Parting Shot"

Meaning: A final remark, typically a cutting one, made by someone at the moment of departure.

Origin: This a variation of Parthian shot, referring to a military manoeuvre in which Parthian troops retreating on horseback turned back to face the enemy and shot while retreating. The Parthians were an ancient race who lived in North-east Persia. They were renowned archers and horsemen and were known for their practice of confusing the enemy by pretending to flee and firing arrows backwards while retreating. In first century BC, Parthia stretched from the Euphrates to the Indus River, covering most of what is now Iran, Iraq and Afghanistan. The Parthians' reputation was well known to English-speaking scholars in the sixteenth and seventeenth centuries; Samuel Butler makes a specific reference to their battle tactic in 1678:

"You wound, like Parthians, while you fly, and kill with a retreating eye." The use of the actual term 'Parthian shot' comes rather later. That is found in 'A Tour in India', the account of a Captain Mundy in 1832. Mundy describes his heroic encounter with a tiger:

"I made a successful Parthian shot with my favourite shotgun, and slew my determined little pursuer."

"Pay Through the Nose"

Meaning: Pay much more than a fair price.

Origin: Though not conclusive experts believe this saying goes back to the days of the Danish invasion of Britain. Ninth-century Danes were particularly strict with their tax laws, especially where 'foreigners' were concerned. They levied a particular tax against the Irish called the 'Nose Tax'; failure to pay was met by harsh punishment – the debtor had his nose slit open.

"Hitting the Sack"

Meaning: Go to bed.

Origin: Mattresses have been around for a long time, the oldest discovered one is fossilised and was found in South Africa, is 77,000 years old and consisted of leaves bound together.

We have been 'hitting the sack' for a long time, the phrase seems to be an adaptation of the older saying 'Hit the hay'. We have been 'Hitting the Hay' since medieval times in the United Kingdom when mattresses were made of cloth sacks filled with hay. There are different theories to why we hit it but the most popular is that we hit it before getting into bed to disturb any bugs that may have decided it was a good resting place for them.

The term 'Hit the hay' isn't as old as you might think in terms of it meaning go to sleep in general, the first printed example of this 1903 in the USA paper the 'Oakland Tribune':

"'Sam' Berger, the Olympic heavyweight, was sleepy and he announced that 'he was going to hit the hay'." 'Hitting the sack' is logical as the hay was within a sack for centuries and is an alternative saying.

"Teacher's Pet"

Meaning: A pupil who has won the teacher's special favour or a person who is treated as a favourite by one in authority.

Origin: The word 'pet' in this case refers to a pampered or spoiled person. The idiom 'teacher's pet' was first seen in print around 1890, though it's safe to assume that it was an epithet hurled around the schoolyard for many years before entering mainstream English.

"Pass with Flying Colours"

Meaning: Pass a test easily or with an exceptionally high score.

Origin: In the past, without the use of modern communication devices, a ship's appearance upon the immediate return to the port could communicate how the crew fared at sea. Ships that were victorious in their endeavours for example, after an encounter with an enemy ship, would sail into port with flags flying from the mastheads. A ship that had been defeated, on the other hand, would be forced to 'strike her colours', or to lower their flags, signifying defeat. This saying created other sayings such as 'sailing under false colours' which was a term given to pirates trying to lure in other ships by displaying friendly colours. This practice was particularly relevant in the Age of Discovery, and prior to the eighteenth century, the phrase was used solely as a nautical term. Later, it began to be used to signify any kind of triumph. The first we see in print of the figurative meaning is in George Farquhar's play, 'The Beaux Stratagem' (1707):

"We came off with flying colours."

"In a Nutshell"

Meaning: To sum something up in just a few words.

Origin: The meaning of the phrase 'in a nutshell' is fairly easy to deduce. Anything that could be written in so few words that it would fit into a nutshell would have to be brief and to the point.

Usage of the phrase in a nutshell was first seen around 77 AD in the work Natural History by Pliny the Elder:

"Cicero hath recorded, that the poem of Homer called the Iliad, written on parchment, was enclosed within a nutshell."

In this instance, the phrase within a nutshell was used to illustrate something that literally happened. Natural History was translated into English in the year 1601 by Philemon Holland. By the 1800s, the idiom in a nutshell was in general use.

"Play It by Ear"

Meaning: Proceed instinctively rather than according to rules or a plan.

Origin: The verb phrase 'play it by ear' has its roots in the sixteenth-century use of the noun 'ear' to mean the ability to recognise sounds and musical intervals, as in they 'have a good ear' according to the Oxford English Dictionary. The earliest example in the Oxford English Dictionary of 'ear' used this way is from 'Pylgrimage of Perfection', a 1526 treatise on English by the monk William Bonde:

"In the psalmody ... haue a good eare." A little over a century later, people began using 'play by ea' to mean play an instrument without the aid of written music. The Oxford English Dictionary's first citation for the newer usage is from 'A Brief Introduction to the Skill of Musick' (1658), by John Playford:

"To learn to play by rote or ear without book." It wasn't until the 1930s, according to a search of book and news databases, that the expression 'play it by ear' developed its modern sense of doing something without a definite plan in mind.

"Read Between the Lines"

Meaning: Look for or discover a meaning that is implied rather than explicitly stated.

Origin: This expression derives from a simple form of cryptography, in which a hidden meaning was conveyed by secreting it between lines of text by means of invisible ink that would become visible when warmed over a candle. It originated in the mid-nineteenth century and soon became used to refer to the deciphering of any coded or unclear form of communication, whether written or not.

The first example found of the phrase in print is from 'The New York Times', August 1862:

"Read between the lines of this puzzling, but important, communication of the British Foreign Secretary."

"Copy Cat"

Meaning: A person who copies another's behaviour, dress or ideas.

Origin: The term 'copycat' refers to the tendency of humans to duplicate the behaviour of others, as expressed in the saying, 'monkey see, monkey do'. The expression is believed to have originated from observing the habits of kittens that learned by imitating the behaviour of their mother.

Why a cat and not a monkey or parrot, which are known more for their imitative behaviour? The term is somewhat logical since 'cat' has been an insult since the medieval period.

Cats were associated with all sorts of evil and mischief. In an early thirteenth century, monastic guidebook for female monks called Ancrene Riwle, for instance, the anonymous author warns ascetics against becoming 'cats of hell', so, it is logical as this term is meant as an insult.

Copycat has been in recorded use since at least 1887 in, Constance Cary Harrison's 'memoir Bar Harbour' : "Our boys say you are a copycat, if you write in anything that's been already printed."

"Toe the Line"

Meaning: Accept the authority, policies or principles of a particular group.

Origin: Its literal sense is to stand or crouch with the toes touching the line, especially at the start of a race or fight. The current meaning is an extension of a figurative usage, to present oneself in readiness for a race, fight, contest or undertaking, which developed from this literal sense. Earlier versions of toeing something can be seen as toeing the mark/ scratch/ crack/ trig but all meant to step up to a line or to conform.

In the Oxford English Dictionary, the earliest quotation for the verb toe in the sense to touch or reach with the toes is from 'The Diverting History of John Bull and Brother Jonathan' (1812), written by the American author James Kirke Paulding (1778–1860) under the pseudonym of Hector Bull-Us:

"He began to think it was high time to toe the mark."

"Jack the Lad"

Meaning: A brash or cocky, young man.

Origin: Though not definitive, the most popular theory is that the 'Jack' in the expression is Jack Sheppard, the eighteenth -century thief who was caught and imprisoned five times but escaped four times, in the process becoming a popular folk hero. He certainly had the credentials to be a real Jack the lad, having made audacious escapes and recklessly carefree robberies. Unfortunately for him, he was guarded day and night during his fifth incarceration and was hanged at Tyburn in November 1724. He was just 22 years old. The earliest use of the expression came in an 1840 song, Jack's the Lad, with such descriptive lines as:

"If ever fellow took delight in swigging, gigging, kissing, drinking, fighting , Damme, I'll be bold to say that Jack's the lad."

"Good as Gold"

Meaning: Completely genuine; also, well behaved.

Origin: Gold isn't particularly known to be either well-behaved or obedient. Originally, 'good' in this saying meant genuine, not counterfeit. The original meaning is recorded in this piece from The Old Bailey records of a trial in October 1827, reported that month in 'The Morning Post':

"Child and the others then went with him to another house in Chancery Lane; they there gave him a paper, which they said was 'as good as gold', and would be paid on Monday next."

The change from the use of 'good', as meaning 'genuine' to 'good', as meaning 'well-behaved' didn't take long. Charles Dickens used it in the latter sense in 'A Christmas Carol', (1843):

"And how did little Tim behave?" asked Mrs Cratchit.
"As good as gold," said Bob, "and better."

"Spreading Yourself Too Thin"

Meaning: To engage in so many activities that one can't perform any of them well.

Origin: This metaphor is based on spreading butter, jam, paint, glue, or some other sticky semiliquid material on a flat surface, in cooking or construction contexts. There is usually a minimum effective thickness for the material being spread, and failing to meet that minimum leaves the material 'spread too thin'.

The oldest recording of this saying is from the 1893 'Report of the Twenty-Third Annual Meeting of the Vermont Dairymen's Association':

"Why, when a man undertakes to spread himself over the whole work embraced in agriculture, even if he is a pretty smart man, he will spread himself too thin."

"Flavour of the Month"

Meaning: A person or thing that enjoys a short period of great popularity.

Origin: The phrase dates back to 1930s USA and originated in the advertising slogans of ice-cream companies . It isn't absolutely clear which company first used this in their campaigns but the earliest known use of the term 'flavour of the month' was by Sealtest ice cream in June 1936:

"If you haven't tried Sealtest Fresh Strawberry Ice Cream, made by Telling's, you're missing a real treat. It's the flavour-of-the month for June, selected by the Sealtest Jury."

"Wearing Your Heart on Your Sleeve"

Meaning: Exposing one's true emotions, making ourselves vulnerable and letting it all hang out.

Origin: The origin of the phrase to wear one's heart on one's sleeve is generally attributed to a jousting custom popular during the Middle Ages. Knights traditionally wore colours or some type of insignia on their arms to signify the ladies for whom they were participating in the jousting tournament.

The term to wear one's heart on one's sleeve was used in a figurative sense by at least 1604 as the term appears in the play 'Othello' written by William Shakespeare:

"But I will wear my heart upon my sleeve / for daws to peck at: I am not what I am."

"The Best of Both Worlds"

Meaning: All the advantages of two different situations and none of the disadvantages.

Origin: This phrase has been a part of English idioms since at least the late 1800s. It is thought to have evolved from the saying 'the best of all possible worlds', which was used in Voltaire's 'Novella Candide', published in 1759.

This phrase was repeated often in literature for the next several decades. The relatively modern phrase 'the best of both worlds' compares only two situations as opposed to the broader comparison implied by Voltaire and subsequent authors.

"Barking Mad"

Meaning: Crazy or insane.

Origin: The meaning for this phrase though not conclusive is thought to be a reference to rabid dogs, barking in their madness. There are many examples of 'barking like a mad dog' in print.

The earliest example found in print is from records of the trial for the murder of a Walter Tricker, in 1867:

"Mrs Hitchins, at the Inquest, says 'It was not ordinary barking. The dogs were barking like tearing mad'."

The first record of it that I can find in print with the exact phrase in reference to something other than dogs is from the USA in a 1927 edition of the Oklahoma newspaper, The Ada Evening News. They reported on the frenetic and borderline insane sport of Auto-polo:

"At 2:30 this afternoon at Park field a half dozen barking mad auto polo, cars will be whirled into action."

"A Bee in One's Bonnet"

Meaning: Someone who is obsessed something and can't stop thinking about it.
Origin: This phrase is thought to have originated in Alexander Douglas's 'Aeneis' (1513):

"Quhat bern be thou in bed with heid full of beis?"

He wrote about someone being in bed with a head full of bees as a euphemism for them not being able to go to sleep with things being on their mind.

Robert Herrick used the idea in the poem Mad Maid's Song in 1648 when he wrote about a woman saying that she would look for the bee that bore her love away in the bonnet of the man whom she loved.

It's not known exactly when, but the phrase seemed to change to 'bee in your bonnet' because of the alliteration of 'bee' and 'bonnet'. The first printed version found, of the exact phrase was published in Thomas De Quincey's Coleridge & Opium-Eating in 1845:

"John Hunter, notwithstanding he had a bee in his bonnet, was really a great man."

"Don't Cry over Spilt Milk"

Meaning: There is no use in being upset over situations that have already happened and cannot be changed.
Origin: While the exact origin of the idiom 'don't cry over spilt milk' isn't exactly known, it is quite likely to have come from faery lore in the middle ages. In the days when people believed strongly in fairies, it was common to lay out a shrine for them, consisting of small quantities of food and drink, particularly of their favourite drink, milk. Whenever milk was spilled, it was considered to be nothing more than a little extra offering to the fairies, and nothing to worry about. This phrase is very old and was first referenced by British historian and writer James Howell in one of his works 'Paramoigraphy' in 1659.

"Lose One's Marbles"

Meaning: Go insane.

Origin: 'Marbles' was coined as a slang term meaning 'wits/common sense', as a reference to the marbles that youngsters play with. An early citation of this figurative usage is found in an August 1886 copy of the 'St Louis Globe-Democrat':

"He has roamed the block all morning like a boy who had lost his marbles."

The expression took a little time to mature and was used in both 'anger' and 'sanity' senses for a few decades. What is common in all the early citations is the sense of loss and the consequent reaction to it. By 1927, the loss of sanity meaning had won out and an edition of American Speech defined the term unambiguously:

"Marbles, he doesn't have all his, mentally deficient. There goes a man who doesn't have all his marbles."

"Harping On"

Meaning: To speak repeatedly and boringly about a topic.

Origin: The term 'harp on' has been known since the sixteenth century. The metaphor is to the tedious repeated plucking of a single string on a harp.

The first use of 'harp on' in print is a quotation from 'A Disputacion of Purgatorye', a 1531 work by the English priest John Frith:

"Se how he harpeth all of one stringe."

Shakespeare also used 'harping on' later, in 'Hamlet' (1602):

"Still harping on, my daughter?"

"April Fool"

Meaning: A trick or hoax on 1 April .

Origin: Although there is no definitive origin, we can trace back some idea of how old this tradition/celebration is. Historians in the UK know it has been celebrated in Britain since at least the nineteenth century. However, an eighteenth-century poem in the UK alludes to an even older theme :

"The first of April some do say,
Is set apart for All Fools' Day,
But why the people call it so,
Nor I, nor they themselves, do know."

An older poem still by English poet Geoffrey Chaucer in the fourteenth century – where a fox plays a prank on a rooster. The poet doesn't actually directly refer to 1 April though. In the poem, he says 32 days 'syn March began', which people have said is '32 days since March began' which would be 1 April .

The earliest concrete records we have about 1 April are from France and Holland in the 1500s and, because of this, people believe that it must have been a northern European tradition that spread to Britain.

It is actually known as April Fish Day in some areas of Europe. People think this is because there are a lot of fish in French streams and rivers around 1 April, and they are easy to catch, like fools, so it soon became a tradition to play tricks on people on 1 April too.

It is still a common trick in France, and elsewhere in Europe, to attach a paper fish to somebody's back on April Fools' Day, and also to give chocolate fish as gifts.

"Have a Taste of Your Own Medicine"

Meaning: Someone should have the same unpleasant experience that they themselves have given to someone.

Origin: The origin of the phrase 'a taste of your own medicine' is very old and comes from Aesop, who lived around 600 BC, in his famous story 'The Cobbler Turned Doctor'.

The story is about a swindler who sells fake medicine, claiming that it can cure anything. When he falls ill, people give him his own medicine, which he knows will not work.

"Pipe Down"

Meaning: Stop talking or be less noisy.

Origin: Although not conclusive, experts believe this derives from sailing ships. Signals were given to the crew by sounding the boatswain's pipe. One such was 'piping down the hammocks' which was the signal to go below decks and retire for the night.

When an officer wanted a sailor to be dismissed below, he would have him 'piped down'. This usage is recorded in Royal Navy workbooks from the eighteenth century. The first example found in print is Gillespie's 'Advice to Commanders and Officers', 1798:

"At four o'clock PM, the hammocks should regularly be piped down."

"Put Your Money Where Your Mouth Is"

Meaning: Someone should do something, especially spend money, to show that they mean what they say.

Origin: This saying is thought to derive from some earlier sayings effectively meaning the same thing, 'put up or shut up'. The earlier examples found first in print are as follows:

"put their money where their faith is" in 'Methodist Episcopal Church Year Book', 1881,

"put your money where your interests are" in 'The Railroad Telegrapher' 1905,

"put your money where your heart is" in 'Publicity and Progress', 1915, and

"put his money where his heart is" in 'The Harvester World', April 1919.

The first example of the saying in its current form is from American sociologist, Howard Odum's 'Rainbow Round My Shoulder: The Blue Trail of Black Ulysses'1928:

"Bet your money, go to hell, put your money where your mouth is, it is down, turn them dam' cards you have fell."

The reasoning is quite obvious, the age of the saying, not so much.

"Through Thick and Thin"

Meaning: Under all circumstances, no matter how difficult.

Origin: This saying is very old and originally related to forest or woodland areas in the UK, in some places the trees are thick and overgrown while in other places it is sparse and easy to navigate.

The saying derived from an old hunting expression 'through thicket and thin wood'. The thicket is a group of trees or bushes that grow close together. The first recorded use of this earlier phrase can be found in Geoffrey Chaucer's 'Canterbury Tales', 1387 – 1400:

"And forth with 'wehee', thurgh thikke and thurgh thenne."

The earliest citation found that uses the exact wording of the current phrase is in Richard Baxter's religious text 'A Saint or a Brute: The Certain Necessity and Excellency of Holiness' (1662):

"Men do fancy a necessity where there is none, yet that will carry them through thick and thin."

"Wait with Bated Breath"

Meaning: To hold one's breath due to suspense, trepidation or fear.

Origin: 'Bated breath' is a phrase first mentioned in Shakespeare's 'The Merchant of Venice' (1596):

"Shall I bend low and in a bondman's key, with bated breath and whispering humbleness."

The word bated, often misspelt as baited, is an abbreviation of the word abated, meaning to lessen in severity or amount. Bated is rarely used on its own as an adjective or verb anymore, but it lingers in the English language in the phrase 'bated breath'.

"Let Sleeping Dogs Lie"

Meaning: Avoid interfering in a situation that is currently causing no problems. Origin: This phrase derives from the long-standing observation that dogs are often unpredictable when they are suddenly disturbed. Although the belief itself may well be much older, Geoffrey Chaucer was the first to put this notion into print, in 'Troilus and Criseyde', circa 1380:

"It is nought good a slepyng hound to wake."

The cautionary phrase was well enough known by the sixteenth century for it to have been included as a proverb in John Heywood's definitive 'A Dialogue conteinyng the nomber in effect of all the Prouerbes in the Englishe tongue' (1546):

"It is euill wakyng of the slepyng dog."

To get to the current wording of the proverb we have to move to the nineteenth century. In December 1822, 'The London Magazine' published a fanciful mariner's yarn entitled 'The Second Tale of Allan Lorburne', which included:
"Let sleeping dogs lie, said the daft man, when he saw the dead hound before him."

"Six of One, Half a Dozen of the Other"

Meaning: Two alternatives that are equivalent or indifferent.

Origin: There is no real mystery behind this phrase in that it is logical, what is interesting is where it is first used in print. It is first recorded in the journal of Ralph Clark who died in 1794.

He was a British Naval Officer who was First Lieutenant on HMS Sirius when the ship was wrecked in March 1790 on a reef at Norfolk Island, in the Pacific Ocean off the east coast of Australia. HMS Sirius was the flagship of the First Fleet, which set out from England in 1787 to establish the first European colony in New South Wales, Australia.

This is what Ralph Clark wrote on Saturday 24 April 1790 when the crew and the convicts were stranded on Norfolk Island:

"There is no difference between Soldier Sailor or Convicts there Six of the one and half a dozen of the other."

"Rat Ars*D"

Meaning: Very drunk.

Origin: This addition to the numerous terms for being drunk entered the language in Britain in the 1990s. It is sometimes shortened just to 'ratted'. It is a follow-on to the earlier phrase 'as pi**ed as a rat'. There wasn't any particular reason to pick on rats, the choice seems almost arbitrary. Other creatures which have been used in similar phrases are newts, ticks or skunks.

The first example found of the term in print is from a piece in the UK paper 'The Guardian', 1992: *"Actually, what really impressed them was that they defied the world even though most of them appeared to be rat-arsed from shortly after breakfast."*

"The Pot Calling the Kettle Black"

Meaning: A person who has accused someone of having a fault has the same fault themselves.

Origin: This phrase originates in Cervantes' 'Don Quixote', or at least in Thomas Shelton's 1620 translation – Cervantes Saavedra's 'History of Don Quixote':

"You are like what is said that the frying-pan said to the kettle, 'Avant, black-browes'."

The first person who is recorded as using the phrase in English was William Penn, the founder of Pennsylvania, in his 'Some Fruits of Solitude' (1693):

"For a Covetous Man to inveigh against Prodigality, an Atheist against Idolatry, a Tyrant against Rebellion, or a Lyer against Forgery, and a Drunkard against Intemperance, is for the Pot to call the Kettle black."

'The pot calling the kettle black' is one of a number of proverbial sayings that guard against hypocrisy and complacency. The context of Penn's use of the expression is one which is similar to 'He who is without sin, cast the first stone'. Another is 'you can't hold with the hare and run with the hounds'.

"It Takes Two to Tango"

Meaning: Both parties involved in a situation or argument are equally responsible for it.

Origin: The phrase refers to the South American dance, the tango, which requires two partners to perform. The saying itself originated from a 1952 song 'Takes Two to Tango' by Al Hoffman and Dick Manning and gained popularity subsequently as an expression.

"Pigs Might Fly"

Meaning: Used ironically to express disbelief.

Origin: This idiom apparently derived from a centuries-old Scottish proverb, though some other references to pigs flying or pigs with wings are more famous. The first printed version, however, appears in the works of Lewis Carroll's 'Alice in Wonderland' (1865):

"Just about as much right," said the Duchess, "as pigs have to fly."

The idiom was said to be brought further to the fore by American literature author John Steinbeck (1902–68) who was told by his professor at school that he would be an author when pigs flew. When he eventually became a novelist, he started to print every book he wrote with the insignia '*Ad astra per alas porci*' meaning 'to the stars on the wings of a pig'. He sometimes added an image of a flying pig, called 'Pigasus'.

Incidentally, a pig finally flew on 4 November 1909, when John Moore-Brabazon, 1st Baron Brabazon of Tara took a small pig with him on board an aeroplane.

"Down in the Dumps"

Meaning: Feeling very sad.

Origin: During the Elizabethan period, a 'dump' was a kind of slow, mournful song or dance.

The earliest printed record of it is in Sir Thomas More's 'A Dialoge of Comforte Against Tribulation' (1529):

"with whiche some of our poore familye bee fallen into suche dumpes."

'Dumps' was used frequently in plays and manuscripts from the sixteenth century onward. Shakespeare used the term several times, for example, in 'The Taming of the Shrew' (1596):

"Why, how now, daughter Katharina, in your dumps?"

The Dutch word 'domp', means 'mental haze or dullness', and the German word 'dumpf', means 'close, heavy, oppressive, gloomy'. And it is thought the word may well derive from one of these words to the English word 'dump' but this is not certain.

The first printed version of 'Down in the dumps' in its full term is in Francis Grose's invaluable *'Classical Dictionary of the Vulgar Tongue'*, 1785:

"DUMPS. Down in the dumps, low-spirited, melancholy."

"Don't Cut Your Nose off to Spite Your Face"

Meaning: To seek retribution against someone else in a manner that is ultimately harmful or disadvantageous to oneself.

Origin: Examples of similar his phrases are known to have been used as early as the twelfth century. It may be associated with the numerous legends of pious women disfiguring themselves in order to protect their Virginity.

One famous example is that of Saint Ebba, the Mother Superior of the Monastery of Coldingham Priory. In AD 867, Viking pirates from Zealand and Uppsala landed in Scotland. When news of the raid reached Saint Ebba, she gathered her nuns together and urged them to disfigure themselves, so that they might be unappealing to the Vikings. The Viking raiders were so disgusted that they burned the entire building to the ground with the nuns inside.

The expression has since become a blanket term for self-destructive actions motivated purely by anger or desire for revenge. In the 1788 edition of Grose's 'Classical Dictionary of the Vulgar Tongue':

"He cut off his nose to be revenged of his face," is defined as 'one who, to be revenged on his neighbour, has materially injured himself'.

The first printed example of the modern saying in its full term can be seen in the London newspaper 'The Guardian', 1861:

"Therefore, if you are disposed to verify the old proverb, and cut off your noses to spite your faces."

"Put Your Best Foot Forward"

Meaning: To try to act as an ideal version of oneself, typically to try to impress others.

Origin: The most common theory for this saying is that the 'best foot' is the right foot, as far back as ancient Rome there are examples of the left side being unlucky or evil. Another example is getting up on the right side of bed and this theory has travelled continents and ages.

We cannot be absolutely conclusive about this but what we can be conclusive about is that as a minimum this saying is hundreds of years old. The earliest example in print is within Shakespeare's play 'King John' (1595):

"Hee is still setting the best foot forward."

Another slight variation can be found shortly after in Sir Thomas Overbury's poem 'A Wife', circa 1613:

"Nay, but make haste, the better foot before."

"If the Shoe Were on the Other Foot"

Meaning: One is experiencing the same, and often bad, things that one caused another person to experience.

Origin: This idiom originated in the mid-1800s. Initially, the exact wording was a little different, 'the boot is on the other leg'. The idea behind this was related to the feeling of discomfort you would have if you put your left shoe on your right foot, and vice versa.

Winston Churchill used this original phrasing famously in 1908 in 'My African Journal':

"Here, the boot is on the other leg, and civilisation is ashamed of her arrangements in the presence of a savage."

"Fall on One's Sword"

Meaning: To accept defeat; to go to extremes to indicate one's defeat.

Origin: The actual practise of committing suicide by falling on one's sword dates back to ancient Rome. Plutarch, a Greek philosopher 350–430 AD, records such a death in 'The Life of Brutus':

"Finally, Brutus spoke to Volumnius himself in Greek, reminding him of their student life, and begged him to grasp his sword with him and help him drive home the blow. And when Volumnius refused, and the rest likewise, grasping with both hands the hilt of his naked sword, he fell upon it."

It is a story of Brutus, Caesar's adopted son, who died 42 BC. This account was translated from Ancient Greek to English in 1918.

The notion was already current in English in the sixteenth century however, and appears in 'The Miles Coverdale Bible' (1535), in an account of the death of Saul:

"Then toke Saul ye swerde, and fell therin. Now whan his wapenbearer sawe that Saul was deed, he fell also vpon his swerde, and dyed with him."

The samurai of Japan who were around from the twelfth century to their abolition in the 1870s were also known for the practice of suicide in this way when faced with capture although the term 'falling on one's sword' was not used.

The figurative meaning is much more recent and a famous example was used widely following the resignation of Lord Peter Carrington, who resigned from his post as Foreign Secretary in the UK for the Thatcher Government in 1982, following Argentina's invasion of the Falkland Islands. He was the last high profile politician in the UK to take personal responsibility in such circumstances.

"Bright-Eyed and Bushy-Tailed"

Meaning: Alert and lively.

Origin: This saying is of American-English origin and comes from the conventional image of a healthy, spirited squirrel or other animal. The following example is the earliest found in print from 'A Bunch of Golden Rod', published in newspaper 'The Daily Picayune' in New Orleans, Louisiana (1888):

"The bushy-tailed, grey squirrels that live in our oak and hickory trees, pretty, soft, bright-eyed little creatures that only take with thankfulness what God made for them, an acorn or a nut."

It is worth pointing out that 'bright eyed' appeared in the late 1500s and 'Bushy tailed' appeared in the mid-1800s individually in print however as an idiom the 1888 example is the earliest version of them found together.

"As Sick as a Parrot"

Meaning: To be very annoyed or disappointed about something.

Origin: Although 'as sick as a parrot' doesn't appear in the Monty Python Dead Parrot sketch, first broadcast in December 1969, it is believed that is where this saying comes from.

There are several 'as dead as' similes, amongst the most notable examples being 'as dead as a dodo' and 'as dead as a doornail'. The Dead Parrot sketch's writers John Cleese and Graham Chapman didn't use either of these either, but they did list as many ways of being dead that they could think of.

That sketch was hugely popular in the UK and many people can quote chunks of it word for word. The idea that a parrot might be an example of something sick began with that sketch at the very end of the 1960s.

"A Storm in a Teacup"

Meaning: A lot of unnecessary anger and worry about a matter that is not important.

Origin: The expression 'A storm in a teacup', is relevant to British English, however, American English uses the slightly different variant of 'a tempest in a teapot'.

The expression can be traced back to the Roman Statesman Cicero in Latin around 100 BC :

"Excitabat enim fluctus in simpulo ut dicitur Gratidius," translated as, "for Gratidius raised a tempest in a ladle, as the saying is."

The expression did not, however, begin to be used in its current form until 1815 when Britain's Lord Chancellor Thurlow referred to an uprising on the Isle of Mann as 'a tempest in a teapot'. It was then in 1838 that the British English version 'a storm in a teacup', was first used in Catherine Sinclair's 'Modern Accomplishments'.

Throughout history, it can be found in other forms such as 'a storm in a wash-basin' but the most frequently used remains 'a storm in a teacup'.

"Daylight Robbery"

Meaning: Blatant and unfair overcharging.

Origin: In 1696, William III of England introduced a property tax which required those living in houses with more than six windows to pay a levy. In order to avoid the tax, house owners would brick up all windows except six. The Window Tax lasted until around 1851, and older houses with bricked-up windows are still a common sight in UK. As the bricked-up windows prevented some rooms from receiving any sunlight, the tax was referred to as daylight robbery.

"Bolt out of the Blue"

Meaning: A sudden or unexpected event.

Origin: There are several forms of this idiom: 'out of the blue' and 'a bolt out of the blue' are two other examples. The earliest citation is from Thomas Carlyle, in 'The French Revolution' (1837):

"Arrestment, sudden really as a bolt out of the Blue, has hit strange victims."

English versions of this expression, however, are thought to derive as translations of the work of the Roman lyric poet Quintus Horatius Flaccus (65–8BC), better known as Horace. A translation from Latin of Horace's 'Ode 34' (1882):

"The sire of heaven on high, by whose fierce bolts the clouds are riven, to-day through an unclouded sky."

Thomas Carlyle was, like many educated men of his era, a classical scholar and would have been well acquainted with Horace's Odes so although the first English version of this saying is 1837 the likelihood is that the saying, or a variation of it actually dates back two millennia.

"A Blow by Blow Account"

Meaning: Giving all the details in the order in which they occurred.

Origin: This expression describes anything that is explained in great detail. It is often seen in sports commentary, a sports presenter will give a 'blow-by-blow account' match so audiences who are not at the game can know what is going on. The phrase has expanded to describe any description of an event given in such detail that the listener can imagine that they are there.

Blow meaning hard hit is a mid-fifteenth-century word, and it likely comes from the Middle Dutch word *blouwen*, which means to beat.

In this sense, 'blow-by-blow' was originally used when giving an account of a prize fight and was first recorded in 1922 in 'The Wireless Age':

"Like a hungry kitten loves its saucer of warm milk, so do radio fans joyfully listen to the blow-by-blow broadcast description of a boxing bout."

"Having an Albatross Around One's Neck"

Meaning: Something that causes you great problems from which you cannot escape.

Origin: This popular idiom is a reference to English poet Samuel Taylor Coleridge's poem 'The Rime of the Ancient Mariner' (1798), in which an albatross is shot by the mariner, bringing feelings of insurmountable guilt upon him and disaster upon his crew:

"Ah! Well-a-day! What evil looks, had I from old and young, Instead of the cross, the Albatross about my neck was hung."

Today these words have been repurposed as an accusatory phrase, often used to describe an unfortunate mishap or mistake.

"Keep It Under Your Hat"

Meaning: To keep something secret.

Origin: Experts believe the origin of this saying lies with medieval archers who would keep spare bowstrings dry under their hats although there is nothing in print to verify this.

In the mid -1800s, the term was used in Britain as an admonishment to keep something in your head, to leave something in your imagination and not bring it to the fore. The oldest example of a very similar phrase is in 'The History of Pendennis' by William Makepeace Thackeray, published in 1848:

"A distinct universe walks about under your hat and under mine."

The idiom travelled to America and underwent a shift in meaning by the 1890s to its current definition, to keep something secret. The most common theory is that this shift in meaning is attributable to Abraham Lincoln's habit of secreting important papers inside the lining of his stovepipe hat. In fact, Lincoln often referred to his hat as his office, again there is no printed evidence of this.

The first time we see the saying in its full usage as we see today is in P. G. Wodehouse's 'Inimitable Jeeves' (1923):

"Despite her humble station, that she kept it under her hat. She meant to spring it on me later."

"Lock, Stock and Barrel"

Meaning: 'All', 'total' or 'everything'.

Origin: Given the antiquity of the three words that make up the phrase and the fact that guns have been in use since at least the Hundred Years' War in 1450, and even earlier in other countries such as China, we might expect it to be very old.

In fact is, it isn't particularly and the earliest use of it appears to come from around the mid-eighteenth century. The earliest use of the phrase in print is from James Ray's 'A Complete history of the Jacobite rebellion' (1752):

"She found my Highland Pistols, which were a Piece of curious Workmanship, the Stock, Lock and Barrel being of polish'd Steel."

This does, however, seem to refer to actual guns and not the metaphoric usage we see today. The first use of the term with its current meaning found is when Rudyard Kipling came close to giving us a definition of the term in 1891, in 'Light That Failed':

"The whole thing, lock, stock, and barrel, isn't worth one big yellow sea-poppy."

"Below the Belt"

Meaning: Disregarding the rules or unfair.

Origin: This expression comes from boxing. It is against the rules for boxers to hit their opponent anywhere below the belt area. So, if a boxer ignored the rules and did this, it would be considered unfair. It later became an idiom for when anyone says something that's uncalled for, their words are like punches that are figuratively hitting 'below the belt'.

The earliest example of this expression in print is the mid-nineteenth century in the 'Bell's Life in London and Sporting Chronicle' newspaper (1841):

"In the second round, Smith, in the act of striking, stumbled forward, and his blew went below the belt of his antagonist."

"On the Ball"

Meaning: Indicating competence, alertness or intelligence.

Origin: The phrase 'on the ball' originated in the sporting arena but relates to the eyes rather than the feet. It is a contraction of the earlier expression 'keep your eye on the ball'.

The phrase is recorded in early records of cricket, golf, croquet and baseball and many people regard baseball as the origin. The earliest citation found in print, however, comes from the English game of rounders.

The English novelist William Kingston wrote 'books for boys', and in 1864 published 'Ernest Bracebridge' or 'Schoolboy Days', which includes this scene:

"Ellis seized the bat with a convulsive clutch… Remembering Ernest's advice, he kept his eye on the ball, and hit it so fairly that he sent it flying away to a considerable distance."

"How Do You Like Them Apples"

Meaning: Used as a way to mock or tease someone after gaining some kind of victory over them.

Origin: 'How do you like them apples' is an expression that is said to have originated during the first World War, when the Allies' anti-tank grenade was colloquially called a 'toffee apple' because of its bulb-like appearance on a stick. The phrase was used as a taunt against the enemy.

"Birds of a Feather"

Meaning: People who are alike, tend to do things together.

Origin: The phrase 'birds of a feather flock together' is at least over 470 years old. It was in use as far back as the mid-sixteenth century. William Turner used a version of this expression in the 'Rescuing of Romish Fox' (1545):

"Byrdes of on kynde and color flok and flye allwayes together."

The first known citation in print of the currently used English version of the phrase appeared in 'The Dictionarie in Spanish and English', which was compiled by the English lexicographer John Minsheu, 1599: 'Birdes of a feather will flocke together'.

At some point after this, birds flocking behaviour started to be applied metaphorically to people who acted in a similar way, and now today we often hear the shortened version of just 'Birds of a feather'.

"Cut to the Chase"

Meaning: Get to the point.

Origin: Films, particularly comedies, often climaxed in chase scenes. Some inexperienced screenwriters or directors would pad the film with unnecessary dialogue, which bored the audience and prolonged the time before the exciting chase scene. 'Cut to the chase' was a phrase used by movie studio executives to mean that the audience shouldn't get bored by the extra dialogue, and that the film should get to the interesting scenes without unnecessary delays.

The first reference to it dates back to the 1920s, just after the first movies with sound began in 'The Jazz Singer' (1927). It is a script direction from Joseph Patrick McEvoy's novel 'Hollywood Girl' (1929):

"Jannings escapes, cut to chase."

"Better the Devil You Know"

Meaning: It may be better to deal with a person or a thing that you are familiar with than to have to deal with a completely new and unknown one.

Origin: This is a shortened version of the old proverb, 'better the devil you know than the devil you don't'. This proverb is related to the Latin proverb, expressed in 1539 in Proverbs or Adages out of Erasmus by R. Taverner,

'Nota res mala, opima', *which means 'an evil thing known is best'.*

It first appeared in print in in its current format in 1857 in the novel 'Barchester Towers' by Anthony Trollope:

"'Better the devil you know than the devil you don't know' is an old saying, and perhaps a true one, but the bishop had not yet realised the truth of it."

"Barnstorming"

Meaning: A flamboyant, energetic and successful. (of a performance or performer)

Origin: Barnstorming earned its name from the early 1920s aerobatic pilots who would land their light planes in fields and use local barns as venues for their impromptu airshows. Paying spectators would gather to watch these daring pilots attempt a variety of dangerous tricks.

Barnstorming is still celebrated today as the foundation of modern airshows. Pilots across the country are passionate about preserving vintage planes and continuing the barnstorming tradition by offering open-cockpit biplane rides to the public.

The Wright Brothers and Glenn Curtiss were known to be the first to have early flying exhibitions and the first 'Barnstormer' was known to be Charles Foster Willard who was taught to fly by Glenn Curtiss in 1909.

"Opening a Can of Worms"

Meaning: To create a complicated situation in which doing something to correct a problem leads to many more problems.

Origin: The exact origin of the phrase is not completely known, but general consensus traces it back to the 1950s in the United States and literal cans of worms. Fisherman used to buy sealed metal cans of earthworms, as opposed to the plastic containers or Styrofoam cups of today.

The earliest documented example of this phrase is found in 1951 edition of the 'Edwardsville Intelligencer' in Illinois,

"The question of command for Middle East defense against Soviet aggression is still regarded as 'a can of worms' at General Eisenhower's SHAPE headquarters here."

Linguists believe that the expression is actually a more modern, Americanised version of the expression 'opening Pandora's Box'.

"Talk the Hind Legs off a Donkey"

Meaning: Unflagging persistence to persuade another by eloquent or charming speech.

Origin: According to the Oxford Dictionary of English Idioms 'talking a horse's hind leg off' was already considered an old expression by 1808 and is mentioned in 'Cobbet's Weekly Political Register' so a form of this idiom may have existed prior to 1800. It is difficult to be sure of its origin.

It is thought to have originated in Ireland, it has been suggested that the expression refers to the fact that horses or donkeys do not usually sit down on their behinds. So, to talk the hind legs off a donkey or horse is to talk so long that the animal becomes exhausted and collapses. The hind legs do not 'fall off' as in the related idiom 'to talk someone's ear off' but they 'lose their legs' as someone who has fainted or collapsed.

"Whipping Boy"

Meaning: A person who is blamed or punished for the faults or incompetence of others.

Origin: Whipping Boy was an established position at the English court during the Tudor and Stuart monarchies of the fifteenth and sixteenth centuries.

This may not have been quite as bad as it sounds. The whipping boys weren't hapless street urchins living a life of torment, but high-born companions to the royal princes. They were educated with the princes and shared many of the privileges of royalty.

The downside was that, if the prince did wrong, the whipping boy was punished. It was considered a form of punishment to the prince that someone he cared about was made to suffer.

The first printed record of the term can be seen in Gilbert Burnet's 'History of his own time' (1715):

"William Murray of the bed-chamber, that had been whipping boy to King Charles the first."

"All the Rage"

Meaning: When something is the height of popularity.

Origin: The word 'rage' comes from the Latin word 'rabies'. It means 'madness'. In effect 'All the rage' is something people are going crazy or wild for.

'The rage' has been used to describe something that is in fashion for more than 200 years. The first example in print is "Europ. Mag. VIII. 473" (1785):

"The favourite phrases, he Rage, the Thing, the Twaddle and the Bore."

Because it is not clear whether 'the rage' was used in its current form the first evidence of the phrase 'all the rage' was in 1834. Lytton, 'Last Days of Pompeii I. i. 173 Sylla' is said to have transported to Italy the worship of the Egyptian Isis. It soon became 'the rage', and was peculiarly in vogue with the Roman ladies.

'All the rage' has been all the rage for between 200 and 250 years.

"Seal the Deal"

Meaning: To make an agreement official.

Origin: The word seal, according to the Oxford English Dictionary, has been in use since the 1200s in the Middles Ages, few people could write, even many nobles couldn't. So, they would 'sign' papers by 'stamping' them with their noble or family seals that had been dipped in ink. As long as they maintained sole possession of such seals, which were hard to manufacture, their 'signatures' couldn't be counterfeited.

The use of 'seal' in this context reflects ancient practice. One easily accessible example, The Biblical book of Jeremiah recounts a land deal as follows:

"I signed the deed, sealed it, got witnesses and weighed the money on scales. Then I took the sealed deed of purchase, containing the terms and conditions and the open copy, and I gave the deed of purchase to Baruch son of Neriah."

"Stick in the Mud"

Meaning: A narrow-minded or un-progressive person.

Origin: The idea behind this expression is thought to originally allude to a vehicle, at the time, a horse drawn carriage, whose wheels were stuck in the mud. Further down the line, this would transfer to a person not willing to move.

It was preceded in the language by earlier versions, for example 'stick in the briers, clay, mire' etc. These were usually applied to people who remained in a difficult situation, either by choice or because they were stuck. 'Stick in the mud' followed these versions but was derived from these earlier versions.

Thomas Cooper's 'Thesaurus', 1565, included an example:

"They beyng accused of extortion and pillage were in muche trouble, or stacke in the bryars."

The first citation of 'Stick in the mud' in print as it is today, is from the eighteenth century. The London newspaper 'The General Evening Post' in November 1733 wrote:

"The Colonel could not swear to him, but the Justice committed him to the same Place with Sutton. George Fluster, alias Stick in the Mud, has made himself an Evidence and impeached the above two Persons."

"Touch Wood"

Meaning: Said after a confident or positive statement, to express a hope for one's good luck to continue.

Origin: The phrase is relatively modern and the oldest citation for the British version of the phrase 'touch wood' dates from 1850, when it was used in the academic correspondence magazine 'Notes and Queries'. This predates the American 'knock on wood' expression.

The most popular theory by far, is that it has its roots in ancient pagan cultures who worshipped and mythologised trees. They believed trees were oracles and were home to spirits and gods. Some pagan cultures would chase evil spirits away by knocking on trees, thereby preventing them from ruining someone's good luck. The Celts, on the other hand, believed this was how you thanked the spirits, or leprechauns, for any good luck you had received. According to Stefan Bechtel's 'The Good Luck Book', the chasing away of spirits probably developed into a superstitious knock over time, which conveys gratitude for any good luck received and acknowledges the spirits' part in it.

The other main theory is that Christianity co-opted an old pagan ritual and incorporated Christian icons. In this theory, the wood becomes the cross Christ was crucified on. When you knock on the wood, you are invoking Christ's protection.

While we cannot be conclusive on this one, the first theory is by far the most popular and we can definitively say it is at least nearly 200 years old but probably much older.

"Let Bygones Be Bygones"

Meaning: To forgive someone for something done or for a disagreement and to forget about it.

Origin: In the fifteenth century, a bygone was simply 'a thing that has gone by', that is, a thing of the past. Shakespeare used it with that meaning in 'The Winters Tale' (1611):

"This satisfaction, the by-gone-day proclaym'd, say this to him."

As time progressed, 'bygones' came to refer specifically to past events that had an unpleasant tinge to them, for example, quarrels or debts. The Scottish churchman Samuel Rutherford recorded that usage of the phrase in a letter during his detention in Aberdeen in 1636. In the letter, he regrets the follies of his youth and acknowledges his debt to God in showing him the error of his ways:

"Pray that byegones betwixt me and my Lord may be byegones."

'Let bygones be bygones' uses both meanings of the word 'bygones' and means, in extended form, 'let the unpleasantness between us become a thing of the past'. Let things that have gone by, go by, in essence.

"Wooden Spoon"

Meaning: A wooden spoon is an award that is given to an individual or team that has come last in a competition.

Origin: The wooden spoon was presented originally at the University of Cambridge as a kind of booby prize awarded by the students to the man who achieved the lowest exam marks but still earned a third-class degree. The term 'wooden spoon' or simply 'the spoon' was also applied to the recipient, and the prize became quite notorious.

The spoons themselves, actually made of wood, grew larger and in later years measured up to five feet long. By tradition, they were dangled in a teasing way from the upstairs balcony in the Senate House, in front of the recipient as he came before the Vice-Chancellor to receive his degree, at least until 1875 when the practice was specifically banned by the University.

The last wooden spoon was awarded to Cuthbert Lempriere-Holthouse, an oarsman of the Lady Margaret Boat Club of St John's College, Cambridge, in 1909 at the graduation ceremony in the University's Senate House.

This 'prize' has been adopted by many sports for the last placed team in the years since its banning in university.

"Whip Round"

Meaning: A collection of contributions of money from a group of people for a particular purpose.

Origin: This expression is very much 'made in England' as it derives from fox hunting, the British Army and Parliament.

In nineteenth-century foxhunts, people were employed to stop the hounds from straying by using whips to keep them in place. Such people became known as 'whippers in' or simply 'whips'. This term has been perpetuated in the British House of Commons where the word 'whip' again does double duty, as it is both the name of the officers whose job it is to guide straying MPs into the voting lobbies.

Later in the nineteenth century, the term began to be used in military Officers' Messes. John Camden Hotten described this in the 1864 edition of 'The Slang Dictionary':

"Whip, after the usual allowance of wine is drunk at mess, those who wish for more put a shilling each into a glass handed round to procure a further supply."

It doesn't take much imagination to see how the process became known as a 'whip round'. Although the process began in officers' messes, it was used more widely whenever a request for group funding was made. The first use of 'whip' in print in this wider context is in Thomas Hughes' novel 'Tom Brown at Oxford', 1861:

"If they would stand a whip of ten shillings a man, they might have a new boat."

"Double Whammy"

Meaning: A two-fold blow or setback.

Origin: A whammy was originally an evil influence or curse. It originated in the USA in the 1940s and is associated with a variety of sports, particularly a bad run of luck in sports. The first reference to it in print is in the Syracuse Herald Journal, 1939:

"Nobody would have suspected that the baseball gods had put the whammy on Myers and Ernie when the ninth opened."

'Double whammy' emerged not long afterwards, as seen here in the 'Oakland Tribune', in 1941, in an interview with the eccentric boxing manager Wirt Ross:

" When I gave my big police dog the evil eye like this, he liked to collapse, went out and nearly got himself killed by the neighbour's pet poodle pooch. Professor Hoffmeister says I don't get the double whammy to put on human beings until Lesson 9."

"Throw Down the Gauntlet"

Meaning: Issue a challenge.

Origin: The phrase dates back to the 1500s. The word 'gauntlet' dates back to the 1300s. It is derived from the French word *'gantelet'*, describing the heavy, metal gloves worn by knights.

They were typically worn into battle and throwing down their gauntlet was the way that they challenged an opponent to a duel. Throwing your glove at the feet of your enemy was seen as an insult. The only way to avenge your honour was to fight the offending party.

The figurative meaning of the phrase dates back the 1700s. Even though a physical gauntlet was no longer used, a challenge was still presented.

"Warts and All"

Meaning: Including features or qualities that are not appealing or attractive.

Origin: This saying is said to have originated in the instructions given by Oliver Cromwell (1599–1658) to the painter Peter Lely to portray him as he truly was, without concealing his blemishes.

This story first appeared in 'Anecdotes of Painting in England', with some account of the principal artist collected by the late Mr George Vertue. This was later published by the English author and politician Horace Walpole in 1763:

"Mr Lely, I desire you would use all your skill to paint my picture truly like me, and not flatter me at all; but remark all these roughnesses, pimples, warts and every thing as you see me, otherwise I never will pay a farthing for it."

The exact wording is suspicious to say the least however, as this has been passed from source to source three times over with it not being recorded until 100 years after Cromwell's death. What we can say is the saying is at least dated 1763 and that it was based on Cromwell, whether he used the words or not.

"Plenty of/More Fish in the Sea"

Meaning: Used to say that there are many more people available for a romantic relationship.

Origin: According to the 'Dictionary of Proverbs', there's plenty of fish in the sea can be found as early as 1573 in the form 'in the main sea, there's a good store of fish'. Originally, the saying was meant about anything lost, not necessarily a love lost.

By 1862, the proverb had morphed into its modern form and was established enough to inspire a classic early American popular song from Stephen Foster, 'There are Plenty of Fish in the Sea'. It is not known where it transformed into the specifics of a lost love.

In 2003, a Vancouver-based dating site alluded to the saying for its free dating website, 'Plenty of Fish', which, as of 2018, claims to be the largest of its kind with over 150 million registered users across the globe.